This is an Indispensable
Spiritual Manual

70 rules of Spiritual Warfare

DR. D. K. OLUKOYA

Seventy Rules of Spiritual Warfare

DR. D. K. OLUKOYA

SEVENTY RULES OF SPIRITUAL WARFARE

ISBN 978-978-8424-24-6
October 2010

Published by:
The Battle Cry Christian Ministries
322, Herbert Macaulay Way, Yaba P. O. Box 12272, Ikeja, Lagos.
email: battlecrysales@mountainoffire.org
Phone: 2348033044239

All Scripture quotation is from the King James Version of the Bible

TABLE OF CONTENTS

THE MYSTERY Of BATTLES

We will start by first looking at the mystery of battles. Judges 4:14-16 say:

And Deborah said unto Barak, Up, for this is the day in which the LORD hath delivered Sisera into thine hand: is not the LORD gone out before thee? So Barak went down from mount Tabor, and ten thousand men after him. And the LORD discomfited Sisera, and all his chariots, and all his host, with the edge of the sword before Barak; so that Sisera lighted down off his chariot, and fled away on his feet. But Barak pursued after the chariots, and after the host, unto Harosheth of the Gentiles: and all the host of Sisera fell upon the edge of the sword; and there was not a man left.

God is not a civilian and life is not a picnic. What we are going through in life is insignificant compared with the arena where war is posing a threat. Many parts of the world have witnessed the ravages of war.

No nation on earth jokes with the strength of her military. Globally, a trillion of the dollars are being spent to defend territorial integrity, prevent external aggression, maintain the super power syndrome, counter hostilities, and quell riots and civil wars in a world that is fast becoming a theater of war.

Wars have become an essential part of human history. Super powers have flexed military muscles. Civil wars have been fought. Wars have taken place between one weak nation and another weak one. In a more frightening dimension, the world witnessed two world wars. As you read these pages some nations are boiling due to wars that have become intractable. New modes of warfare have emerged.

COMPLEX BATTLE PATTERNS

There are now different patterns of warfare:

1. Biological warfare.
2. Revolutionary war.
3. Civil war.
4. Religious war.
5. Atomic or nuclear warfare.
6. Internecine war.
7. Guerrilla warfare.
8. Germ or bacteriological warfare.
9. Land mine warfare.
10. Trench warfare.
11. Aerial warfare.
12. Combat warfare.
13. Space warfare.
14. Air warfare.

THE CONSEQUENCES

Many nations in Africa expend a huge budget on overseas military training and the acquisition of weapons. The world has become a boiling, militarized arena. The entire globe has found itself in the cannon's mouth. Billions of dollars have been expended on arms and ammunition.

People who have found themselves in the frightening jaw of war know that warfare is not a child's play. Casualties of warfare are legion. Innocent children, pregnant women and people who do not know their left hand from their right hand have suddenly become enmeshed in wars which they know nothing about. Much property has been lost, several lives have been driven to unexpected graves. Consequently, many have been traumatized. A lot of military and non-military personnel have shed their blood simply because a nation or a community is at war.

THIS IS WAR

If this can go on in the physical, what with spiritual war? The Bible has made us to know that physical and spiritual warfare are incomparable. The amount of human, psychological and material wastage that we have witnessed will weigh nothing when compared with the colossal, tragic and wanting destructions that play themselves out on daily basis on the invisible but tangible field of spiritual battles. The Bible has jolted us into consciousness on the more damaging effects of spiritual warfare.

Jeremiah 12:5 says:

If thou hast run with the footmen, and they have wearied thee, then how canst thou contend with horses? and if in the land of peace, wherein thou trustedst, they wearied thee, then how wilt thou do in the swelling of Jordan?

If the world has become weary through incessant physical warfare, how would it cope with conflicts with powers that bite without remnants? If running with foot soldiers have left multitudes devastated what will happen in the case of contending with a group of blood sucking demons? If the world has become tired in the land of relative peace what will happen with the swelling of Jordan occasioned by wicked hostilities emanating from principalities, powers and spiritual wickedness? The totality of the global warfare which we have known since the world began is just an infinitesimal fraction of the degree of hotness of the battle that goes on in the spiritual realm.

THE BATTLE ARENA

Physical warfare is real and threatening, but spiritual warfare is more frightening.. Surveying the entire landscape of life, the Ephesians 6:10-13 declares:

Finally, my brethren, be strong in the Lord, and in the power of his might. Put on the whole armour of God, that ye may be able to stand against the wiles of the devil. For we wrestle not against flesh and blood, but against principalities, against powers, against the rulers of the darkness of this world, against spiritual wickedness in high places. Wherefore take unto you the whole armour of God, that ye may be able to withstand in the evil day, and having done all, to stand.

There is no denying the fact that life is one long stretch of unending battles. Most of the time the battle begins in the womb. As soon as a child is born, the battle moves to another gear. The story of man is the story of repeated battles. If you have read biographies, you would have discovered that there is no man whose life has been void of battles. Jacob confessed that he fought one battle after another.

Genesis 47:9 says:

And Jacob said unto Pharaoh, The days of the years of my pilgrimage are an hundred and thirty years: few and evil have the days of the years of my life been, and have not attained unto the days of the years of the life of my fathers in the days of their pilgrimage.

NAGGING BATTLES

He made it crystal clear that he had seen evil days marked by nagging battles.

Job also had a story to tell in Job 14:1:

Man that is born of a woman is of few days, and full of trouble.

The battles which Job faced compelled him to confess that the existence of man is only a few days full of troubles. Battles were written in bold letters in the life of Moses. As an innocent baby he was almost killed by Pharaoh, Egypt's reigning the monarch.

Part of his battles confined him to a trackless desert for 40 years.

Exodus 1:22 says:

And Pharaoh charged all his people, saying, Every son that is born ye shall cast into the river, and every daughter ye shall save alive.

Again, when he meant no harm he killed an Egyptian as a show of nationalism.

Exodus 2:11-15 says:

And it came to pass in those days, when Moses was grown, that he went out unto his brethren, and looked on their burdens: and he spied an Egyptian smiting an Hebrew, one of his brethren. And he looked this way and that way, and when he saw that there was no man, he slew the Egyptian, and hid him in the sand. And when he went out the second day, behold, two men of the Hebrews strove together: and he said to him that did the wrong, Wherefore smitest thou thy fellow? And he said, Who made thee a prince and a judge over us? Intendest thou to kill me, as thou killedst the Egyptian? And Moses feared, and said, Surely this thing is known. Now when Pharaoh heard this thing, he sought to slay Moses. But Moses fled from the face of Pharaoh, and dwelt in the land of Midian: and he sat down by a well.

Joseph was mesmerised by his own battles.

Genesis 37:17-24 says:

And the man said, They are departed hence; for I heard them say, Let us go to Dothan. And Joseph went after his brethren, and found them in Dothan. And when they saw him afar off, even before he came near unto them, they conspired against him to slay him. And they said one to another, Behold, this dreamer cometh. Come now therefore, and let us slay him, and cast him into some pit, and we will say, Some evil beast hath devoured him: and we shall see what will become of his dreams. And Reuben heard it, and he delivered him out of their hands; and said, Let us not kill him. And Reuben said unto them, Shed no blood, but cast him into this pit that is in the wilderness, and lay no hand upon him; that he might rid him out of their hands, to deliver him to his father again. And it came to pass, when Joseph was come unto his brethren, that they stript Joseph out of his coat, his coat

of many colours that was on him; And they took him, and cast him into a pit: and the pit was empty, there was no water in it.

On one occasion he was left to die in a pit. He recorded another milestone battle when it appeared as if he was left to rot in jail.

Genesis 39:20 says:

And Joseph's master took him, and put him into the prison, a place where the king's prisoners were bound: and he was there in the prison.

Paul the Apostle also grappled with one battle after another.

2 Cor. 11:23-29 says:

Are they ministers of Christ? (I speak as a fool) I am more; in labours more abundant, in stripes above measure, in prisons more frequent, in deaths oft. Of the Jews five times received I forty stripes save one. Thrice was I beaten with rods, once was I stoned, thrice I suffered shipwreck, a night and a day I have been in the deep; In journeyings often, in perils of waters, in perils of robbers, in perils by mine own countrymen, in perils by the heathen, in perils in the city, in perils in the wilderness, in perils in the sea, in perils among false brethren; In weariness and painfulness, in watchings often, in hunger and thirst, in fastings often, in cold and nakedness. Beside those things that are without, that which cometh upon me daily, the care of all the churches. Who is weak, and I am not weak? who is offended, and I burn not?

You have your own battles as much as I have mine. But I have good news for you: Victory is sure

1Cor 15:57 says:

But thanks be to God, which giveth us the victory through our Lord Jesus Christ.

1. Let every battle in the heavenlies be won in favour of the angels conveying my blessings today, in Jesus' name.
2. Lord, let the wicked be shaken out of my heavens, in the name of Jesus.
3. Sun, as you are coming out today, uproot every wickedness targeted against my life, in the name of Jesus.
4. I programme blessings into the sun for my life, in the name of Jesus.

5. Sun, I have risen before you and I cancel every evil programme projected into you by wicked powers against my life, in the name of Jesus.
6. You this day, you will not destroy my prosperity, in the name of Jesus.
7. Sun, moon and stars, carry your afflictions back to the sender and release them against him, in Jesus' name.
8. God, arise and uproot everything You have not planted in the heavenlies that is working against me, in Jesus' name.
9. Let the wicked be shaken out from the ends of the earth, in the name of Jesus.
10. Sun, as you come forth, uproot all the wickedness that has come against my life, in the name of Jesus.
11. I programme blessings into the sun, the moon and the stars for my life today, in the name of Jesus.
12. Sun, cancel every daily evil programme drawn against me, in the name of Jesus.
13. Sun, torment every enemy of the kingdom of God in my life, in the name of Jesus.
14. Those who spend the night pulling me down, O sun, throw them away, in the name of Jesus.
15. Elements, you shall not hurt me, in Jesus' name.
16. Heavenlies, you shall not steal from my life, in the name of Jesus.
17. I establish the power of God over the heavenlies, in the name of Jesus.
18. Sun, moon and stars, fight against the stronghold of witchcraft targeted at me today, in Jesus' name.
19. Heavenlies, torment every unrepentant enemy to submission, in Jesus' name.
20. Heavens, fight against the stronghold of witchcraft, in the name of Jesus.
21. Every wicked altar in the heavenlies, I throw you down.

WHEN YOU MUST FIGHT

We continue by considering when you must fight. Warfare is inevitable. We must fight because life itself is a battle. We must fight because forces are set against us. We must fight because if we fold our hands the enemy remains an incurable fighter. We must fight because the enemy is a stranger to mercy. We must fight because if we refuse to fight the enemy will bare his fangs and demonstrate terrible wickedness. We must fight because warfare goes on whether we are ready to fight or not. We must fight because the enemy is a lawless fighter. We need to fight in order to possess our possessions

Obadiah 17 says:

But upon mount Zion shall be deliverance, and there shall be holiness; and the house of Jacob shall possess their possessions.

We must fight because the God whom we serve is a Man of war

Exodus 15:3 says:

The LORD is a man of war: the LORD is his name.

We must go into battle because Jesus, our Commander in-chief, is standing gallantly on the field of battle in readiness to lead us into victory. The following are lines from an ancient hymn reminding us the battles we are called to fights:

Christ our royal Master, stands against the foe.

Forward into battle, loud the anthem raise.

Onward Christian soldiers, marching as to war.

Looking unto Jesus, who is gone before us.

IMPORTANCE OF WARFARE

Warfare is an intrinsic component of Christian living. Christian living not backed up by spiritual warfare is a weak religion. Jesus fought against the powers of hell in the Garden of Gethsemane. The battle was so fierce that it is recorded that His sweet was falling down like drops of blood.

Luke 22:43-44 says:

And there appeared an angel unto him from heaven, strengthening him. And being in an agony he prayed more earnestly: and his sweat was as it were great drops of blood falling down to the ground.

What kind of prayer will anyone pray and sweat would be mixed with blood? Warfare prayer. What pattern of prayer will magnetise angelic assistance? Warfare prayer. What type of prayer would someone pray and great drops of blood would be oozing out from the pores of the skin? Warfare prayers.

Let us cast our minds back to the Old Testament What transpired when Jacob wrestled with the angel till the breaking of the day? Spiritual warfare!

Gen 32:24-30 says:

And Jacob was left alone; and there wrestled a man with him until the breaking of the day. And when he saw that he prevailed not against him, he touched the hollow of his thigh; and the hollow of Jacob's thigh was out of joint, as he wrestled with him. And he said, Let me go, for the day breaketh. And he said, I will not let thee go, except thou bless me. And he said unto him, What is thy name? And he said, Jacob. And he said, Thy name shall be

called no more Jacob, but Israel: for as a prince hast thou power with God and with men, and hast prevailed. And Jacob asked him, and said, Tell me, I pray thee, thy name. And he said, Wherefore is it that thou dost ask after my name? And he blessed him there. And Jacob called the name of the place Peniel: for I have seen God face to face, and my life is preserved.

What type of prayer do you expect a man to pray and have the hollow of his thigh dislocated? Warfare prayers.

From the foregoing, it is crystal dear that warfare prayer plays an important role as far as the victorious life in concerned.

Prayer Points

1. Oh heaven, fight for me against powers sitting on my glory, in the name of Jesus.
2. Any satanic agents using their evil hands to torment my life, be tormented, in the name of Jesus.
3. Let the home of the wicked be cut off,. in the name of Jesus.
4. Every satanic home speaking against my greatness, be silenced, in the name of Jesus.
5. Every demon in charge of satanic home, be arrested, in the name of Jesus.
6. Every spiritual embargo placed upon my destiny, be consumed by fire, in the name of Jesus.
7. I will take my position among the rulers of this world, in the name of Jesus.
8. Every evil conspiracy against my glory, be shattered unto desolation, in the name of Jesus.
9. Every power that says I will not make it, scatter by fire, in the name of Jesus.
10. Every satanic conspiracy against my glory, be shattered unto desolation, in the name of Jesus.

11. Every power increasing against me, be pulled down by fire, in the name of Jesus.
12. All those that gathered against me, be put to shame, in the name of Jesus.
13. Holy Spirit, arise in Your majesty and touch every area of my life, in the name of Jesus.
14. Anointing of glory, enter my life, in the name of Jesus
15. Spirit of impossibility, jump out of my life, in the name of Jesus.
16. Anointing of prosperity, overshadow my life, in the name of Jesus.
17. Evil wounds and injuries in my spirit and body, be healed, in the name of Jesus.

HIDDEN BATTLES

We go on to consider hidden battles. The worst condition anyone on earth can go through is to remain ignorant concerning the realities of the battles of life. To prepare yourself for the mysteries to be revealed in this chapter take the following prayer points.

Prayer points

1. Power of sorrow, hear the word of the Lord: let my destiny go, in the name of Jesus.
2. Thou power of unprofitable delay, you are a liar. Die, in the name of Jesus.
3. You wicked personality, following me about, I cut you off, in the name of Jesus.
4. Let the hold of the enemy over my life break, in the name of Jesus

(SING A SONG OF PRAISE)

5. Anyone who has accepted witchcraft for my sake, be destroyed by fire, in the name of Jesus
6. Aggressive elements targeted to disgrace me, die, in the name of Jesus.

7. Every evil power that has established authority in my family, your time is up, I cancel the authority, die, in the name of Jesus.
8. Every biting demon, be silenced, in the mighty name of Jesus.
9. Every alignment of witches positioned in my direction, be scattered, in Jesus' name.
10. Every power fighting me unto desolation, die, in the mighty name of Jesus.
11. I remove my name from the register of the wasted, in the mighty name of Jesus.

THE BATTLES OF LIFE

As human beings, we must understand and believe that life is but a battle. Everyone living on earth does have an enemy. Unbelief does not stop the harassment of the enemy. Everyone with a colourful destiny has an enemy who is ready to destroy that destiny and stop the star from shining. The book of Job tells us: "Man that is born of a woman is of a few days and is full of trouble." This tells us that the world is not a place to dance and play but a place to watch and pray.

Some people are in the midst of their battles and many have won so many battles. Battle implies "war" - spiritual warfare. Wherever there is something right, the powers of darkness projects wrong. They want to exchange light with darkness, joy for sadness and peace for war. Every time strange and satanic spirits contest for the human heart, spirit and soul. There are about 10 great passages that must be seriously considered in this subject. The Bible also presents itself as a military book. It has military terminologies scattered across its pages. Let us start with Exodus 15:3 which says:

The LORD is a man of war: the LORD is his name.

This tells us that even God Almighty is not a civilian but a soldier. This implies that a true child of God cannot afford to behave or act like a civilian. But in all attributes, he must behave like a soldier, just like the Father. If the world was a playground, God would not be called "the Lord of host" or the "Lord who is a man of war."

Eph 6:12 says:

For we wrestle not against flesh and blood, but against principalities, against powers, against the rulers of the darkness of this world, against spiritual wickedness in high places.

WE WRESTLE

The word "wrestle" in the above passage is a very harsh word. Originally, it refers to struggling, hand to hand fighting, extreme conflict, hazardous and deadly fighting, brutal and barbaric fighting which goes on except one of the parties surrenders or dies.

1 Tim 6:12 says:

Fight the good fight of faith, lay hold on eternal life, whereunto thou art also called, and hast professed a good profession before many witnesses.

The "fight" in the above passage is not a suggested opinion but a command that must be followed to the letter.

Psalm 144:1 says:

Blessed be the LORD my strength, which teacheth my hands to war, and my fingers to fight.

THE MILITARY INSTRUCTOR

God, here, presents Himself as an instructor in warfare. He teaches people how to fight and conquer.

1 Cor 9:26 says:

I therefore so run, not as uncertainly; so fight I, not as one that beateth the air.

This implies that one can fight as if one was fighting the air. The fighting may be seen like a drug without efficacy. But the Bible commands that we fight on.

Rev. 12:7-8 says:

And there was war in heaven: Michael and his angels fought against the

dragon; and the dragon fought and his angels, And prevailed not; neither was their place found any more in heaven.

As you read this book, it is my prayer that any dragon power harassing your destiny shall be arrested, in the mighty name of Jesus.

2 Timothy 2:5 says:

And if a man also strive for masteries, yet is he not crowned, except he strive lawfully.

THE RULES

This simply implies that striving and fighting have binding laws and rules that must be followed if we must achieve the desired success.

2 Cor 10:4 says:

(For the weapons of our warfare are not carnal, but mighty through God to the pulling down of strong holds.)

This teaches us that we are involved in warfare and that we must make use of the appropriate weapons for that warfare; and the weapons are not carnal or physical; they are spiritual.

1 Tim 1:18 says:

This charge I commit unto thee, son Timothy, according to the prophecies which went before on thee, that thou by them mightest war a good warfare.

We can war a good warfare. Certain charges or rules were given to Timothy by which he was to fight a good warfare. Many people are fighting and many are praying but are not getting the desired result because they are misusing the rules of the warfare. This leads to frustration.

In Deuteronomy chapter 20, God gave some instructions to the Israelites to observe whenever they were going to war. Those rules led them to a triumphant end. They also achieved success in whatsoever war they fought. These rules are still useful in our time.

Deut 20:1-8 says:

When thou goest out to battle against thine enemies, and seest horses, and chariots, and a people more than thou, be not afraid of them: for the

LORD thy God is with thee, which brought thee up out of the land of Egypt. And it shall be, when ye are come nigh unto the battle, that the priest shall approach and speak unto the people, And shall say unto them, Hear, O Israel, ye approach this day unto battle against your enemies: let not your hearts faint, fear not, and do not tremble, neither be ye terrified because of them; For the LORD your God is he that goeth with you, to fight for you against your enemies, to save you. And the officers shall speak unto the people, saying, What man is there that hath built a new house, and hath not dedicated it? let him go and return to his house, lest he die in the battle, and another man dedicate it. And what man is he that hath planted a vineyard, and hath not yet eaten of it? let him also go and return unto his house, lest he die in the battle, and another man eat of it. And what man is there that hath betrothed a wife, and hath not taken her? let him go and return unto his house, lest he die in the battle, and another man take her. And the officers shall speak further unto the people, and they shall say, What man is there that is fearful and fainthearted? let him go and return unto his house, lest his brethren's heart faint as well as his heart.

DEADLY DISTRACTIONS

The bottom-line is that we all have wars to fight. Some people are doing well, some are failing woefully and some have been buried alive at the war front. From the above passage, we can deduce that God recognises that there are certain things that cause distractions on the field of battle. You must deal with them to win the war. Distraction remains one of the most disastrous enemies of man. It can lead to the total defeat of a man and even a nation. Some people have been tied down, some have fallen from great heights, some have been dethroned from glorious thrones. Some have been disgraced, some have been caged. An embargo has been placed on the career and success of many.

A lot of people have been stopped. Some have been limited by strange powers and many have been placed under financial embargo. Many have escaped from bondage and are led further into other bondage. This teaches us that the world is a battle ground and not an Olympic field or a recreation or picnic ground. It becomes more traumatising when your blood is fighting against you. It is my prayer that every form of warfare arrayed against you shall be scattered unto desolation, in the mighty name of Jesus. Amen

HIDDEN BATTLES

There is a story of someone who got married and after the wedding the couple were given a small girl to live with them. That was the beginning of their battles. When the wife got pregnant there was war every night. Somebody came physically and dragged the baby out. The woman could not understand what happened. For several months they suffered until they were able to know where the battle came from. It is my prayer that as you read this book, every hidden battle in your life shall cease right now, in the mighty name of Jesus.

I once prayed for a young girl who was around the age of 10 and she told me strange things. Before she began saying those things, immediately we began praying, she suddenly began to speak fluent Latin and anytime the prayer stopped, she stopped speaking the language. This was very strange. She later said that the brain of her older brother had been converted to saw-dust and that he would never excel in any examination again in his life. She said that the last one he passed was the very last he was going to pass. I asked her what also happened to her father's business and she said that anytime he collected a cheque, she took it to a witchcraft meeting and immediately it arrived there, no matter the value of the money and no matter what he did with it, he would eventually lose and get into trouble. It is my earnest prayer that every form of battle you are facing that has been assigned to disgrace and demote you shall be scattered unto desolation, in the mighty name of Jesus.

Prayer points

1. Let every battle in the heavenlies be won in favour of the angels conveying my blessings, in the name of Jesus.
2. Let every satanic law programmed into my life be terminated, in the name of Jesus.
3. Let every evil ancestral law programmed into my genes be terminated, in the name of Jesus.

4. Let my prayers release angelic intervention in my favour, in the name of Jesus.
5. I receive the anointing to disgrace satanic arrows, in Jesus' name.
6. I cut off every supply of food to my problems, in the name of Jesus
7. Let thunder from the Lord destroy every evil altar constructed against me, in the name of Jesus.
8. Lord, release me from known and unknown curses.
9. I rebuke every power working against the soundness of my mind, in the name of Jesus.
10. I seal the rebuke with the blood of Jesus.
11. Let every untamed enemy be tamed by the Holy Ghost, in the name of Jesus.
12. I break every evil padlock put upon my business, in Jesus' name.
13. Let the blood of Jesus rub off evil creams and ointments put upon my body, in the name of Jesus.
14. Let every witchcraft meeting summoned for my sake be scattered unto desolation, in the name of Jesus.
15. Let every chain of satanic accusation be shattered, in Jesus' name.
16. Let every resistance to my breakthroughs crumble, in Jesus' name.

WHY MUST WE FIGHT

We continue by considering why we must fight.

Spiritual warfare is a must for all believers. We are soldiers of Christ. We must be militant and aggressive.

2 Tim 2:3-5 says:

Thou therefore endure hardness, as a good soldier of Jesus Christ. No man that warreth entangleth himself with the affairs of this life; that he may please him who hath chosen him to be a soldier. And if a man also strive for masteries, yet is he not crowned, except he strive lawfully.

THE FOLLOWING ARE THE REASONS YOU MUST FIGHT.

1. To possess your possessions.

Obadiah 1:17 says:

But upon mount Zion shall be deliverance, and there shall be holiness; and the house of Jacob shall possess their possessions.

Since their birth, many people have never had a clue to what they should enjoy. Many have been allocated to where they will never rise. Ninety per cent of success comes as a result of correct positioning. The enemy has repositioned some people so that they will never succeed.

2. To enlarge your coasts.

Isaiah 54:2-3 says: Enlarge the place of thy tent, and let them stretch forth the curtains of thine habitations: spare not, lengthen thy cords, and strengthen thy stakes; For thou shalt break forth on the right hand and on the left; and thy seed shall inherit the Gentiles, and make the desolate cities to be inhabited.

If you do not fight, you coasts remain small and susceptible to attacks and might even be taken away from you.

3. To fight to defend yourself and your territory.

Eph. 6:10-14 says:

Finally, my brethren, be strong in the Lord, and in the power of his might. Put on the whole armour of God, that ye may be able to stand against the wiles of the devil. For we wrestle not against flesh and blood, but against principalities, against powers, against the rulers of the darkness of this world, against spiritual wickedness in high places. Wherefore take unto you the whole armour of God, that ye may be able to withstand in the evil day, and having done all, to stand. Stand therefore, having your loins girt about with truth, and having on the breastplate of righteousness.

It has been said and unanimously agreed upon that the best defence is attack. Do not wait until you are attacked before you start fighting. Take the battle to the enemy's gates.

4. To recover what the enemy has stolen from you.

I Tim. 6:12 says:

Fight the good fight of faith, lay hold on eternal life, whereunto thou art also called, and hast professed a good profession before many witnesses.

The Bible says that we should fight a fight of faith

5. To fulfil your destiny.

Matt. 13:28 says:

He said unto them, An enemy hath done this. The servants said unto him, Wilt thou then that we go and gather them up?

Some destinies have been truncated and damaged because people would not fight. The enemy is ready to destroy your destiny except you are ready to fight.

6. Because the only language the enemy understands is the language of violence.

Matt. 11:12 says:

And from the days of John the Baptist until now the kingdom of heaven suffereth violence, and the violent take it by force.

7. Because you either fight or perish. When you face an enemy, you make use of your most potent weapon.

8. Because, whether you live or not, war has been declared against you.

9. Because sometimes peace and justice cannot be achieved through peace but through violence. That is to say, sometimes when there is no war, there will be no peace.

10. Because the world contains many ruthless and wicked entities.

Psalm 74:20 says:

Have respect unto the covenant: for the dark places of the earth are full of the habitations of cruelty.

11. Because there are some unrepentant enemies that will refuse any peaceful reconciliation means.

Psalm 3:6-7 says:

I will not be afraid of ten thousands of people, that have set themselves against me round about. Arise, O LORD; save me, O my God: for thou hast smitten all mine enemies upon the cheek bone; thou hast broken the teeth of the ungodly.

12. Because it has been ordered from heaven that we fight.

Eph 6:12-13 says:

For we wrestle not against flesh and blood, but against principalities, against powers, against the rulers of the darkness of this world, against

spiritual wickedness in high places. Wherefore take unto you the whole armour of God, that ye may be able to withstand in the evil day, and having done all, to stand.

You either fight or perish.

13. Because there are plenty of persistent and unrepentant enemies fighting against you.

Psalm 149:5-9 says:

Let the saints be joyful in glory: let them sing aloud upon their beds. Let the high praises of God be in their mouth, and a twoedged sword in their hand; To execute vengeance upon the heathen, and punishments upon the people; To bind their kings with chains, and their nobles with fetters of iron; To execute upon them the judgment written: this honour have all his saints. Praise ye the LORD.

14. You need to fight to deliver yourself from oppression.

Eccl 7:7 says: **Surely oppression maketh a wise man mad; and a gift destroyeth the heart.**

15. To pull down the servant ridding the horse of your destiny.

Eccl 10:7 says:

I have seen servants upon horses, and princes walking as servants upon the earth.

16. To key into the mystery of opposition. Opposition is the ladder to honour and the gateway to glory. There must be opposition. And if you run away from it, you will certainly miss your possession and position. There would not have been a David if there was no Goliath. It was the opposition of Goliath that made David a popular personality. It is my prayer that every Goliath's opposition assigned against you shall be disgraced.

Prayer points

1. I bind and put to flight all the spirits of fear, anxiety and discouragement, in the name of Jesus.
2. Lord, let divine wisdom fall upon all who are supporting me in these

matters.

3. I break the backbone of the spirits of conspiracy and treachery, in the name of Jesus.
4. Lord, hammer my matter into the minds of those who will assist me so that they do not suffer from demonic loss of memory.
5. I paralyse the hand work of household enemies and envious agents in this matter, in the name of Jesus.
6. You devil, take your leg away from the top of my finances, in the mighty name of Jesus.
7. Let the fire of the Holy Spirit purge my life from any evil mark put upon me, in the name of Jesus.
8. Let the Lord confuse the tongues of those gathered to do me harm, after the order of the builders of the Tower of Babel, in the name of Jesus.
9. Let my adversaries make mistakes that will advance my cause, in the name of Jesus.
10. I command every evil power and vessel sitting on my rights and goodness to be violently overthrown, in the name of Jesus.
11. I pursue, overtake and recover my properties from the hands of spiritual Egyptians, in the name of Jesus.
12. Let every counsel, plan, desire, expectation, imagination, device and activity of the enemy against this case be rendered null and void, in the name of Jesus.
13. I terminate every journey into bondage and unfruitfulness designed for me by the enemies of my soul, in the name of Jesus.
14. I bind every money-consuming demon attached to my finances, in the name of Jesus.
15. I refuse to be tossed about by any demonic device of the enemy to delay my miracle, in the name of Jesus.

RULES OF SPIRITUAL WARFARE

Spiritual warfare has rules. When you follow them you will always experience victory. We shall be looking at 70 tested and proven rules from this chapter to chapter 16.

RULE NUMBER 1 - YOU MUST KNOW THE GOD YOU SERVE

Warfare Scriptures

Daniel 11:32 says:

And such as do wickedly against the covenant shall he corrupt by flatteries: but the people that do know their God shall be strong, and do exploits.

Psalm 62:11 says: **God hath spoken once; twice have I heard this; that power belongeth unto God.**

You must understand that power belongs to God and that His power is awesome and cannot be contested. There is absolutely no one that can battle with the Lord. His power is absolute. You must be able to stand like Shedrach, Meshaek and Abednego.

There is a story of a young man who was captured along with other people by ritual killers. As the ritualists were killing the other people, cutting off their body parts, ranging from the head, the breast, the genitals and other parts, the young man started praying as it was getting to his turn. As he was praying the ritualists started getting confused. Then they discovered that there was a problem and asked the young man to stop praying. But he remembered the words of Esther, and determined that if he perished, so be it, he roared in violent tongues and the ritual killers scattered. An unknown man in flowing white gown dragged him away from the scene. When he became conscious he found himself at the University of Lagos. He had demonstrated the power of God in action.

There was a peculiar case that took place in one of our branches abroad. A 30-year-old lady had her womb surgically removed because of cancer. To the glory of God, she got pregnant and had a baby girl.

Prayer points

1. Every warfare prepared against my peace, I command panic upon you, in the name of Jesus.
2. Every warfare prepared against my peace, I command havoc upon you, in the name of Jesus.
3. Every warfare prepared against my peace, I command chaos upon you, in the name of Jesus.
4. Every warfare prepared against my peace, I command pandemonium upon you, in the name of Jesus.
5. Every warfare prepared against my peace, I command disaster upon you, in the name of Jesus.
6. Every warfare prepared against my peace, I command confusion upon you, in the name of Jesus.
7. Every warfare prepared against my peace, I command spiritual acid upon you, in the name of Jesus.
8. Every warfare prepared against my peace, I command destruction upon you, in the name of Jesus.

9. Every warfare prepared against my peace, I command hornets of the Lord upon you, in the name of Jesus.
10. Every warfare prepared against my peace, I command disaster upon you, in the name of Jesus.
11. I frustrate every satanic verdict issued against me, in the name of Jesus.
12. Let the finger, vengeance, terror, anger, fear, wrath, hatred and burning judgement of God be released against my full-time enemies, in the name of Jesus.
13. Every power preventing the perfect will of God from being done in my life, receive failure and defeat, in the name of Jesus.
14. Let the warring angels and the Spirit of God arise and scatter every evil gathering sponsored against me, in the name of Jesus.

RULE NUMBER 2 - YOU MUST KNOW YOURSELF

Warfare Scriptures

2 Chr. 2:6 says:

But who is able to build him an house, seeing the heaven and heaven of heavens cannot contain him? who am I then, that I should build him an house, save only to burn sacrifice before him?

2 Sam 7:18 says:

Then went king David in, and sat before the LORD, and he said, Who am I, O Lord GOD? and what is my house, that thou hast brought me hitherto?

I Sam 18:18 says:

And David said unto Saul, Who am I? and what is my life, or my father's family in Israel, that I should be son in law to the king?

I Chr. 29:14 says:

But who am I, and what is my people, that we should be able to offer so willingly after this sort? for all things come of thee, and of thine own have we given thee.

Ex. 3:11 says:

And Moses said unto God, Who am I, that I should go unto Pharaoh, and that I should bring forth the children of Israel out of Egypt?

2 Cor. 13:5 says:

Examine yourselves, whether ye be in the faith; prove your own selves. Know ye not your own selves, how that Jesus Christ is in you, except ye be reprobates?

You need to know yourself very well. There are some things that you are doing that hinder prayer. Are you ready to stop. There was a case when the great apostle, Joseph Ayo Babalola, went to hold a crusade in a certain village. As was his custom to bless a river after every crusade he held, he blessed a river and warned that anyone who had a negative spirit must not drink or bath in it. A certain religious and respected "Mother in Israel," who was a witch, thought it was only a joke. She knew she was not clean but she drank the water. A force lifted her up, smashed her on the floor and made her naked. Everybody saw that she had two reproductive organs (male and female) and she was disgraced. Nobody should joke with the power of God.

There is a story of a sister who was having great troubles and she took up her Bible, opened to Psalm 35 and began to pray. She discovered that the more she prayed the more uncomfortable she became. She was praying against her enemy, yet she was the culprit.

Prayer Pints

1. Divine immunity against every power of darkness, locate me now, in the name of Jesus.
2. Ladders of darkness in my life, die, in the name of Jesus.

RULE NUMBER 3 - KNOW YOUR ENEMY

Warfare Scriptures

2 Cor. 2:11 says:

Lest Satan should get an advantage of us: for we are not ignorant of his devices.

Do not fight an unknown enemy.

Everybody ought to know whom Satan is, and war should be declared and directed towards the enemy. If you do not know your enemy, you may take your enemy for your friend. Lack of adequate knowledge about the enemy is a disaster. Some people started their battle the day they came into the world. Some started theirs from the womb. The greatest tragedy is for your battle to escort you to the grave. It is my prayer that whatsoever battle you are fighting shall be scattered now, in the mighty name of Jesus.

The success of a man's life is measured by computing the battles against the enemy he wins and the ones he loses. Gone are the days when people buy prayers. In war, people get wounded and unless the wounds are well-treated they can damage the quality of the people's lives. There are psychological problems and serious casualties in wars. Some people die, some are captured and taken to the enemy's camp and tortured. If you live your life without God, it opens you up for attacks from the enemy.

Prayer Points

1. As I go into this warfare, I receive a covering of the blood of Jesus. I stay in the strong tower which is the name of the Lord.
2. I receive God's unction and power upon my tongue, in the name of Jesus.
3. I forbid any satanic retaliation against me and my family, in the name of Jesus.
4. In this battle, I shall fight and win. I shall be a victor and not a victim, in the name of Jesus
5. I put on the helmet of salvation, the belt of truth, the breastplate of righteousness, I wear the shoe of the gospel and I take the shield of faith

as I go into this territorial intercession and warfare, in the name of Jesus.

6. I bind and rebuke the princes and powers in charge of this (mention the name of the city), in the name of Jesus
7. I command the fire of God on all the idols, traditions, sacrifices and rituals on this land, in the name of Jesus
8. I break all the agreements made between the people of this city and satan, in the name of Jesus.
9. I decide and claim this city for God, in the name of Jesus
10. Let the presence, dominion, authority and blessings of God be experienced in this city, in the name of Jesus.

RULE NUMBER 4 - DO NOT DEPEND ON HUMAN RESOURCES BUT HEAVENLY RESOURCES

Warfare Scriptures

2 Cor 10:4-5 says:

(For the weapons of our warfare are not carnal, but mighty through God to the pulling down of strong holds;) Casting down imaginations, and every high thing that exalteth itself against the knowledge of God, and bringing into captivity every thought to the obedience of Christ.

The resources of God are greater than that of any human resources that can be imagined. It is wrong to depend on human resources. It leads to failure. A believer must know how to use spiritual weapons.

RULE NUMBER 5 - FEAR GOD MORE THAN THE ENEMY

These days, it is rampant to see Christians misbehaving and fighting in churches which implies that the fear of God is fading from the house of God. There was a church where a policeman had to use tear-gas to settle scuffles. As the fear of God is being eroded from the church, believers are becoming more susceptible to being taken captive. If we must succeed and remain victorious, the fear of God must come back to the heart of Christians.

Prayer Points

1. The spirit of the fear of death, depart from my life, in the name of Jesus.
2. The evil door keepers of insulin, loose your hold, in the name of Jesus.
3. Every power destroying insulin in my body, I bind you and cast you out, in the name of Jesus.
4. Every power hindering the co–ordination between my brain and my mouth, I bind you and cast you out, in the name of Jesus.
5. Every spirit of torment, release me, in the name of Jesus.
6. Every power attacking my blood sugar, loose your hold, in the name of Jesus:
7. I break every curse of eating and drinking blood from 10 generations backward on both sides of my family' lines, in the name of Jesus.
8. Every door opened to diabetes, loose your hold, in Jesus' name.
9. Every inherited blood disease, loose your hold, in Jesus' name.
10. All bloodline curses, be broken, in the name of Jesus.
11. Every curse breaking the skin of my body unrighteously, be broken, in the name of Jesus.
12. I bind every demon in my pancreas and I cast them out, in the name of Jesus.
13. Any power affecting my vision, I bind you, in the name of Jesus:
14. Every satanic arrow in my blood vessel, come out by fire, in the name of Jesus.
15. Every demon of stroke, come out with all your roots, in the name of Jesus.
16. Every spirit of confusion, loose your hold, in the name of Jesus.
17. Anything inhibiting my ability to read and meditate on the word of God, be uprooted, in the name of Jesus.

RULE NUMBER 6 - EMPLOY MIGHTY, ACCURATE SPIRITUAL WEAPONS

Warfare Scriptures

Eph 6:12-17 says:

For we wrestle not against flesh and blood, but against principalities, against powers, against the rulers of the darkness of this world, against spiritual wickedness in high places. Wherefore take unto you the whole armour of God, that ye may be able to withstand in the evil day, and having done all, to stand. Stand therefore, having your loins girt about with truth, and having on the breastplate of righteousness; And your feet shod with the preparation of the gospel of peace; Above all, taking the shield of faith, wherewith ye shall be able to quench all the fiery darts of the wicked. And take the helmet of salvation, and the sword of the Spirit, which is the word of God.

2 Cor. 10:4-6 says:

(For the weapons of our warfare are not carnal, but mighty through God to the pulling down of strong holds;) Casting down imaginations, and every high thing that exalteth itself against the knowledge of God, and bringing into captivity every thought to the obedience of Christ; And having in a readiness to revenge all disobedience, when your obedience is fulfilled.

Jer. 51:20 says:

Thou art my battle axe and weapons of war: for with thee will I break in pieces the nations, and with thee will I destroy kingdoms.

There are various spiritual weapons in God's armory. Locate the appropriate ones for the battle you are fighting and begin to use them effectively.

Prayer Points

1. Let all the weapons and devices of my oppressors and tormentors be rendered impotent, in the name of Jesus.
2. Let the fire of God destroy the power operating any spiritual vehicle working against me, in the name of Jesus.

3. Let all the evil advice given against my favour crash and disintegrate, in the name of Jesus.
4. Let all the eaters of flesh and drinkers of blood stumble and fall, in the name of Jesus.
5. I command all stubborn pursuers to pursue themselves, in the name of Jesus.
6. Let the wind, the sun and the moon run contrary to every demonic presence in my environment, in the name of Jesus.
7. You devourers, vanish from my labour, in the name of Jesus.
8. Let every tree planted by fear in my life dry up to the roots, in the name of Jesus.
9. I cancel all enchantments, curses and spells that are against me, in the name of Jesus.
10. Let all iron-like curses break, in the name of Jesus.
11. Let divine tongues of fire roast any evil tongue against me,. in the name of Jesus.
12. Let all pronouncement uttered against me by poisonous tongues be nullified, in the name of Jesus.
13. I cut myself off from every territorial spirit, in Jesus' name.
14. I loose myself from any power of witchcraft and bewitchment, in the name of Jesus.
15. I loose myself from every satanic bondage, in the name of Jesus.
16. I cancel the power of all curses upon my head, in Jesus' name.
17. I bind the strongman over my life, in the name of Jesus.

RULE NUMBER 7 - EXPLOIT THE ENEMY'S WEAKNESSES

James 2:19 says:

Thou believest that there is one God; thou doest well: the devils also believe, and tremble.

James 4:7 says:

Submit yourselves therefore to God. Resist the devil, and he will flee from you.

Every Goliath has an unprotected forehead. Every enemy has a weakness. You must locate the weakness and use it to your advantage.

Prayer Points

1. I fire back all satanic arrows of weakness, in prayer and Bible reading, in the name of Jesus.
2. I fire back all satanic arrows of business failure, in Jesus' name.
3. I fire back all evil arrows from the household enemy, in the name of Jesus.
4. I fire back all evil arrows from my unfriendly friends, in Jesus' name.
5. Power of God, bring to life all my good benefits that satanic arrows have paralysed, in the name of Jesus.
6. I cover my life and all my belongings from satanic arrows by the blood of Jesus.
7. Thank the Lord that the gate of hell shall not prevail against your life.
8. I order confusion and scattering of tongues against all wicked associations militating against the peace of my life, in Jesus' name.
9. Let the wisdom of all evil counsellors in my life be rendered to nothing, in the name of Jesus.
10. Lord, cause an explosion of your power in my handiwork.
11. Let my life be barricaded by the edge of fire, and let me be soaked and covered with the blood of Jesus.
12. Lord, smite all evil tongues rising against me by the cheekbones and break the jaw of the devil.
13. Let every handwriting contrary to my peace receive intensive disgrace, in the name of Jesus.
14. Let every decision taken against me by the wicked be rendered null and void, in the name of Jesus.

15. I fire back every demonic arrow targeted at me and my family, in the name of Jesus.
16. I break every spiritual mirror and monitor fashioned against me, in the name of Jesus.
17. Pray in the spirit for 10 to 15 minutes.
18. I bind and render to nothing all the strongmen that are currently troubling my life, in the name of Jesus.

STRATEGY FOR VICTORY

The role of strategy in spiritual warfare cannot be over-emphasised. In this chapter, we shall continue our journey into the realm of rules of spiritual warfare.

RULE NUMBER 8 - YOU MUST LEARN HOW TO FIGHT AND WHEN TO FLEE

Mark 1:35 says:

And in the morning, rising up a great while before day, he went out, and departed into a solitary place, and there prayed.

Running gives you time to recover. You must be able to know how to retreat to refire. You must never fight out of pride when you know that you have become weak. When you run the enemy is deceived to assume that you have given up or surrendered. But that gives you time for a devasting counter-attack and to subsequently destroy the enemy.

- **Prayer Points**

1. Thank the Lord because He is the Lord of hosts and the Man of war.
2. I claim victory over every adversary in this court case, in the name of Jesus.
3. I bind and paralyse the strongman employed or delegated to disgrace me, in the name of Jesus.
4. Let all the affairs of my life be too hot for any evil power to manipulate, in the name of Jesus.
5. Lord, grant me and my lawyer supernatural wisdom to subdue all opposition.
6. Lord, let it be impossible for my adversary to subdue the truth in this matter, in the name of Jesus.
7. Lord, let me find favour in the sight of those who are responsible for judging this case.
8. I close every negative door that the enemy may want to open, using this case, in the name of Jesus.
9. You satanic agents, I command you to clear out from the pathway to my victory in this matter, in the name of Jesus.
10. I cancel any demonic decision and expectation concerning this case, in the name of Jesus.
11. Father, make it possible for me to find favour in the sight of the judge, in the name of Jesus.
12. Lord, let me find favour, compassion and loving kindness with the jury, in the name of Jesus.
13. Let all the demonic obstacles that have been established in the heart of anyone against my prosperity be destroyed, in the name of Jesus.
14. Lord, give all the parties concerned dreams, visions and restlessness that would advance my cause.
15. I command my money being caged by the enemy to be completely released, in the name of Jesus.

16. I bind and put to flight all the spirits of fear, anxiety and discouragement, in the name of Jesus.

RULE NUMBER 9 - LEARN TO CUT OFF THE ENEMY'S SUPPLY SYSTEM

Exodus 7:10-12 says:

And Moses and Aaron went in unto Pharaoh, and they did so as the LORD had commanded: and Aaron cast down his rod before Pharaoh, and before his servants, and it became a serpent. Then Pharaoh also called the wise men and the sorcerers: now the magicians of Egypt, they also did in like manner with their enchantments. For they cast down every man his rod, and they became serpents: but Aaron's rod swallowed up their rods.

Exodus 8:16-18 says:

And the LORD said unto Moses, Say unto Aaron, Stretch out thy rod, and smite the dust of the land, that it may become lice throughout all the land of Egypt. And they did so; for Aaron stretched out his hand with his rod, and smote the dust of the earth, and it became lice in man, and in beast; all the dust of the land became lice throughout all the land of Egypt. And the magicians did so with their enchantments to bring forth lice, but they could not: so there were lice upon man, and upon beast.

This is fighting the way Moses fought. Moses fought the idols behind the powers of Egypt. They were handicapped when their spiritual supply was cut off. Unto every enemy there is a spiritual power backing him up and he has a power base. When he is destabilised from the power base, he becomes powerless.

Prayer points

1. Let the home of the wicked be cut off, in the name of Jesus.
2. Every satanic home speaking against my greatness, be silenced, in the name of Jesus.
3. Every demon in charge of satanic home, be arrested, in the name of

Jesus.

4. Every spiritual embargo placed upon my destiny, be consumed by fire, in the name of Jesus.
5. I will take my position among the rulers of this world, in the name of Jesus.
6. Every evil conspiracy against my glory, be shattered unto desolation, in the name of Jesus.
7. Every power that says I will not make it, scatter by fire, in the name of Jesus.
8. Every satanic conspiracy against my glory, be shattered unto desolation, in the name of Jesus.
9. Every power increasing against me, be pulled down by fire, in the name of Jesus.
10. All those who are gathered against me, be put to shame, in the name of Jesus.
11. Holy Spirit, arise in Your majesty and touch every area of my life, in the name of Jesus.
12. Anointing of glory, enter my life, in the name of Jesus
13. Spirit of impossibility, jump out of my life, in the name of Jesus.
14. Anointing of prosperity, overshadow my life, in the name of Jesus.
15. Evil wounds and injuries in my spirit and body, be healed, in the name of Jesus.
16. Let the fly hovering over my spirit and body die, in the name of Jesus.
17. Fire of God, heal all my spiritual injuries, in the name of Jesus.

RULE NUMBER 10 - ANY SIN IN YOUR LIFE WILL STRENGTHEN THE ENEMIES AGAINST YOU

Num. 32:23 says:

But if ye will not do so, behold, ye have sinned against the LORD: and be sure your sin will find you out.

Sin opens you to attacks and strengthens the enemy against you. It is a terrible tragedy and wherever it is, heaven is far away.

Prayer Points

1. Lord, let the spirit that flees from sin incubate my life.
2. I claim all my rights now, in the name of Jesus.
3. Holy Ghost, grant me a glimpse of Your glory now, in Jesus' name.
4. Holy Ghost, quicken me, in the name of Jesus.
5. I release myself from any inherited bondage that is negatively affecting my career, in Jesus' name.
6. Lord send Your axe of fire to the foundation of my life and destroy every evil plantation attacking the success of my career, in Jesus' name.
7. Let the blood of Jesus flush out from my system every inherited satanic deposit, in Jesus' name.
8. I command all foundational strongmen attached to me to be paralysed, in the name of Jesus.
9. Let any rod of the wicked rising up against my career be rendered impotent for my sake, in the name of Jesus.
10. I cancel the consequences of any evil local name attached to my person, in the name of Jesus.
11. I release myself from every evil domination and control, in the name of Jesus.
12. Let every evil imagination against my career wither from the source, in the name of Jesus,
13. Let the destructive plan of the enemies aimed against my career blow up in their faces, in the name of Jesus.
14. Let my point of ridicule be converted to a source of miracle, in Jesus' name.
15. Let all powers sponsoring evil decisions against me be disgraced, in the name of Jesus. .

16. Let the stubborn strongman delegated against me and my career fall down to the ground and become impotent, in the name of Jesus.

RULE NUMBER 11 - TAKE TIME TO EXAMINE PREVAILING SITUATIONS WELL BEFORE STARTING

Luke 14:28-32 says:

For which of you, intending to build a tower, sitteth not down first, and counteth the cost, whether he have sufficient to finish it? Lest haply, after he hath laid the foundation, and is not able to finish it, all that behold it begin to mock him, Saying, This man began to build, and was not able to finish. Or what king, going to make war against another king, sitteth not down first, and consulteth whether he be able with ten thousand to meet him that cometh against him with twenty thousand? Or else, while the other is yet a great way off, he sendeth an ambassage, and desireth conditions of peace.

You must look at the situation very well and search thoroughly at what you want to wage war against before you start a war.

Prayer Points

1. Thou Man of war, save me out of the hands of the wicked midwives, in the name of Jesus.
2. I render every weapon fashioned against my pregnancy impotent, in the name of Jesus.
3. Lord, overthrow every Egyptian working against me in the midst of the sea, in the name of Jesus.
4. I close down every satanic broadcasting station fashioned against my pregnancy, in the name of Jesus.
5. I will see the great work of the Lord as I am delivered of my children safely, in the name of Jesus.
6. I refuse to harbour any pregnancy killer in any department of my life, in the name of Jesus.
7. Every horse and the rider in my womb, family or office, be thrown into

the sea of forgetfulness, in the name of Jesus.

8. I bind every spirit of error assigned against my pregnancy, in the name of Jesus.
9. Lord, send Your light before me to drive powers behind miscarriages away from my womb and life, in the name of Jesus.
10. I bind the spirit of almost there; you will no more operate in my life, in the name of Jesus.
11. I cast out every power casting out my children, in the name of Jesus.
12. I break every grip and hold of witchcraft over my pregnancy, in the name of Jesus.
13. From today, I shall not cast away my young, in the name of Jesus.
14. I paralyse every opposition to my pregnancy, in the name of Jesus.
15. I will fulfil the number of the days of this pregnancy, in the name of Jesus.
16. Any member of my family, reporting my pregnancy to the evil ones, receive the slap of the angels of God, in Jesus' name.
17. I shall not cast out my pregnancy before delivery, in the name of Jesus.
18. Every territorial demon working against my marriage, receive the thunder fire of God, in Jesus' name.

RULE NUMBER 12 - SEARCH FOR YOUR ADVANTAGES

I John 4:4 says:

Ye are of God, little children, and have overcome them: because greater is he that is in you, than he that is in the world.

Col. 1:28 says:

To whom God would make known what is the riches of the glory of this mystery among the Gentiles; which is Christ in you, the hope of glory.

Every believer has a lot of advantages over the enemy.

Prayer Points

1. Lord, reveal to me those things that give my enemies advantage over me.
2. Lord, let my fellowship with You become greater.
3. I draw upon heavenly resources today, in the name of Jesus.
4. Lord, enable me to become the person You created me to be.
5. I surrender myself completely in every area of my life, in the name of Jesus.
6. I stand against every satanic operation hindering my prayers, in the name of Jesus.
7. Satan, I refuse your involvement in my prayer life, in Jesus' name.
8. Satan, I command you to leave my presence with all your demons, in the name of Jesus.
9. I bring the blood of the Lord Jesus Christ between me and you satan.
10. Father Lord, open my eyes to see how great You are, in the name of Jesus.
11. I declare that satan and his wicked spirits are under my feet, in the name of Jesus.
12. I claim the victory of the Cross for my life today, in Jesus' name.
13. Every satanic foothold in my life, be dismantled by fire, in the name of Jesus.
14. I put off all forms of weakness, in the name of Jesus.
15. Lord Jesus, come into my life by fire.
16. Lord Jesus, break down every idol and cast them out every foe.
17. Every wicked spirit planning to rob me of the will of God, fall down and die, in the name of Jesus.
18. I tear down the stronghold of satan against my life, in the name of Jesus.
19. I smash every plan of satan formed against me, in Jesus' name.
20. I smash the stronghold of satan formed against my body, in the name of Jesus.

21. Lord, let me be the kind of person that would please you.

RULE NUMBER 13 - ANALYZE THE STRENGTHS AND WEAKNESSES OF YOUR ENEMY

Pro. 20:18 says:

Every purpose is established by counsel: and with good advice make war.

You have to study the enemy to know where he is strong and where he is weak and utilise the knowledge effectively.

Prayer Points

1. I fire back all satanic arrows of weakness in prayer and Bible reading, in the name of Jesus.
2. I fire back all satanic arrows of business failure, in Jesus' name.
3. I fire back all evil arrows from household enemies, in the name of Jesus.
4. I fire back all evil arrows from my unfriendly friends, in Jesus' name.
5. Power of God, bring to life all my good benefits that satanic arrows have paralysed, in the name of Jesus
6. I cover my life and all my belongings from satanic arrows by the blood of Jesus.
7. Thank the Lord that the gate of hell shall not prevail against your life.
8. I order confusion and scattering of tongues against all wicked associations militating against the peace of my life, in Jesus' name.
9. Let the wisdom of all evil counsellors in my life be rendered to nothing, in the name of Jesus.
10. Lord, cause an explosion of Your power in my handiwork.
11. Let my life be barricaded by the edge of fire, and let me be soaked and covered with the blood of Jesus.
12. Lord, smite all evil tongues rising against me by the cheekbones and

break the jaw of the devil.

13. Let every hand writing contrary to my peace receive intensive disgrace, in the name of Jesus.

RULE NUMBER 14 - KNOW YOUR WEAPONS

Eph. 6:11-18 says:

Put on the whole armour of God, that ye may be able to stand against the wiles of the devil. For we wrestle not against flesh and blood, but against principalities, against powers, against the rulers of the darkness of this world, against spiritual wickedness in high places. Wherefore take unto you the whole armour of God, that ye may be able to withstand in the evil day, and having done all, to stand. Stand therefore, having your loins girt about with truth, and having on the breastplate of righteousness; And your feet shod with the preparation of the gospel of peace; Above all, taking the shield of faith, wherewith ye shall be able to quench all the fiery darts of the wicked. And take the helmet of salvation, and the sword of the Spirit, which is the word of God: Praying always with all prayer and supplication in the Spirit, and watching thereunto with all perseverance and supplication for all saints.

As a believer, you must know all your spiritual weapons. You must know the blood of Jesus, the word of God, the fire of the Holy Spirit, the weapon of brimstone and fire, the whirl wind and the East wind. You must settle down and know these weapons and their uses. This explains why David took five stones when he went to attack Goliath.

Prayer Points

1. I nullify all spiritual weapons being used to slow down my progress, in the name of Jesus.
2. I cancel all strongholds that the spirit of fear has built in me, in the name of Jesus.
3. Lord, begin to baptize every area of my life with Your dumbfounding miracles.

4. I nullify every evil effect of fear in my life, in the name of Jesus.
5. Lord, give me the spirit of boldness.
6. Let all the powers that shake off God's blessings in my life be removed and be destroyed, in the name of Jesus.
7. I place myself now under the Cross of Jesus.
8. I cover myself with the precious blood of Jesus.
9. I surround myself to the light of Christ.
10. The devil will not interfere with the Lord's work in my life, in the name of Jesus.
11. I put on God's armour to resist the devil tactics, in Jesus' name.
12. Lord, reveal to me any way that satan has a hold on my life.
13. I claim back any territory of my life handed over to satan, in the name of Jesus.
14. I bind all forces of evil in the air, fire, water and ground being set in motion against my life, in the name of Jesus.
15. I forbid any spirit from any source from harming me in any way, in the name of Jesus.
16. I reject every spirit of seduction, in the name of Jesus.
17. I refuse to let sin have dominion over me, in the name of Jesus.
18. I reject every satanic promise on any department of my life, in the name of Jesus.
19. Let the powers setting themselves up in opposition to me be paralysed, in the name of Jesus.

RULE NUMBER 15 - YOUR ENEMIES WILL ALWAYS TAKE ADVANTAGE OF YOUR DISTRESS

Pro. 24:10 says:

If thou faint in the day of adversity, thy strength is small.

Phil..4:6 says:

Be careful for nothing; but in every thing by prayer and supplication with thanksgiving let your requests be made known unto God.

Every distress or panic of the believer is an advantage to the devil. Once you panic, you start losing the battle. The Bible warns that you should be careful for nothing. There was an occult man who had entered into 16 different cults. He lived in a house with a woman who happened to be a believer. The woman never knew that her prayer was always disturbing him. He vowed to deal with the woman by attacking her son. Early one particular morning, the boy began to convulse and the woman began to pray. The situation continued without the woman knowing that the man had a nail he was always hammering into a particular place on a wall. She kept praying and the nail kept jumping out.

At a time, the man visited the woman and gave her a concoction to give to the boy to drink but the woman refused. If the boy had taken the concoction, he would have died. The man continued the nailing. At a point, the face of an old man appeared on his wall and warned him never to hit the nail again, that instead he should do away with all his fetish powers and go to the woman and asked to be taken to the church. When he demanded who the old man was, the old man replied that he was the Ancient of Days. The man ran to the woman and today, he is born again. If the woman had allowed the panic syndrome, she would have accepted the concoction and her son would have been killed. Panic kills a believer faster than anything you can ever imagine.

I Sam 17:1-11, 24 says:

Now the Philistines gathered together their armies to battle, and were gathered together at Shochoh, which belongeth to Judah, and pitched between Shochoh and Azekah, in Ephesdammim. And Saul and the men of Israel were gathered together, and pitched by the valley of Elah, and set the battle in array against the Philistines. And the Philistines stood on a mountain on the one side, and Israel stood on a mountain on the other side: and there was a valley between them. And there went out a champion out of the camp of the Philistines, named Goliath, of Gath, whose height was six cubits and a span. And he had an helmet of brass upon his head, and he was armed with a coat of mail; and the weight of the coat was five thousand shekels of brass. And he had greaves of brass upon his legs, and a target of

brass between his shoulders. And the staff of his spear was like a weaver's beam; and his spear's head weighed six hundred shekels of iron: and one bearing a shield went before him. And he stood and cried unto the armies of Israel, and said unto them, Why are ye come out to set your battle in array? am not I a Philistine, and ye servants to Saul? choose you a man for you, and let him come down to me. If he be able to fight with me, and to kill me, then will we be your servants: but if I prevail against him, and kill him, then shall ye be our servants, and serve us. And the Philistine said, I defy the armies of Israel this day; give me a man, that we may fight together. When Saul and all Israel heard those words of the Philistine, they were dismayed, and greatly afraid. 24. And all the men of Israel, when they saw the man, fled from him, and were sore afraid.

Prayer Points

1. Every enemy that will not let me go easily, I bring the judgment of death against you, in Jesus' name.
2. This year, my blessing will not sink, in the name of Jesus.
3. Let the spirit of salvation fall upon my family, in Jesus' name.
4. Every grip of the evil consequences of the ancestral worship of my forefathers' god over my life and ministry, break by fire, in Jesus' name.
5. Every covenant with water spirits, desert spirits, witchcraft spirits, spirits in evil sacred trees, spirits inside / under sacred rocks / hills, family gods, evil family guardian spirits, family / village serpentine spirits, masquerade spirits and inherited spirit husband / wives, be broken by the blood of Jesus.
6. Every unconscious evil soul-tie and covenant with the spirits of my dead grandfather, grandmother, occult uncles, aunties, custodian of family gods/oracles/shrines, be broken by the blood of Jesus.
7. Every decision, vow or promise made by my forefathers contrary to my divine destiny, loose your hold by fire, in the name of Jesus.
8. Every legal ground that ancestral guardian spirits have in my life, be destroyed by the blood of Jesus.

9. Every generational curse of God resulting from the sin of idolatry of my forefathers, loose your hold, in Jesus' name.
10. Every ancestral evil altar prospering against me, be dashed against the Rock of Ages, in the name of Jesus.
11. Every ancestral placenta manipulation of my life, be reversed, in the name of Jesus.
12. Every evil ancestral life pattern, designed for me through vows, promises and covenants, be reversed, in Jesus' name.

STRATEGIC WARFARE

There are secrets of victory which you need to understand. They will make you an uncommon overcomer. The rules of spiritual warfare to be examined in this chapter are very crucial as far as overwhelming victory is concerned

RULE NUMBER 16 ATTACK THE STRATEGY OF THE ENEMY

Job 5:12 says:

He disappointeth the devices of the crafty, so that their hands cannot perform their enterprise.

2 Cor 2:11 says:

Lest Satan should get an advantage of us: for we are not ignorant of his devices.

The enemies always follow a particular pathway to attack a believer. You must detect and attack their strategies.

Prayer Points

1. Satanic attacks against my life in my dreams, be converted to victory, in

Jesus' name.

2. Let all rivers, trees, forests, evil companions, evil pursuers, pictures of dead relatives, snakes, spirit husbands, spirit wives, masquerades manipulated against me in the dream be completely destroyed by the power in the blood of the Lord Jesus.
3. I command every evil plantation in my life, come out with all your roots, in the name of Jesus! (Lay your hands on your stomach and keep repeating the emphasised area.)
4. I withdraw my health from the hands of the bondwoman and her children, in Jesus' name
5. You will not squander my divine opportunities, in the name of Jesus.
6. I dismantle any power working against me, in the name of Jesus.
7. I refuse to lock the door of blessing against myself, in the name of Jesus.
8. I refuse to be a wandering star, in the name of Jesus.
9. I refuse to appear to disappear, in the name of Jesus.
10. Let the riches of the Gentiles be transferred to me, in the name of Jesus.
11. Angels of God, pursue every enemy of my prosperity to destruction, in Jesus' name.
12. Let the sword of Goliath of poverty working against me, die, in the name of Jesus.
13. Let wealth change hands in my life, in the name of Jesus.
14. Lord, make a hole in the roof for my prosperity in the name of Jesus.
15. Let the yoke of poverty upon my life be dashed to piece, in the name of Jesus.

RULE NUMBER 17 CARRY OUT SURPRISE ATTACKS

Josh 8:1-17 says:

And the LORD said unto Joshua, Fear not, neither be thou dismayed: take all the people of war with thee, and arise, go up to Ai: see, I have given into thy hand the king of Ai, and his people, and his city, and his land: And thou shalt do to Ai and her king as thou didst unto Jericho and her king: only the spoil thereof, and the cattle thereof, shall ye take for a prey unto yourselves: lay thee an ambush for the city behind it. So Joshua arose, and all the people of war, to go up against Ai: and Joshua chose out thirty thousand mighty men of valour, and sent them away by night. And he commanded them, saying, Behold, ye shall lie in wait against the city, even behind the city: go not very far from the city, but be ye all ready: And I, and all the people that are with me, will approach unto the city: and it shall come to pass, when they come out against us, as at the first, that we will flee before them, (For they will come out after us) till we have drawn them from the city; for they will say, They flee before us, as at the first: therefore we will flee before them. Then ye shall rise up from the ambush, and seize upon the city: for the LORD your God will deliver it into your hand. And it shall be, when ye have taken the city, that ye shall set the city on fire: according to the commandment of the LORD shall ye do. See, I have commanded you. Joshua therefore sent them forth: and they went to lie in ambush, and abode between Bethel and Ai, on the west side of Ai: but Joshua lodged that night among the people. And Joshua rose up early in the morning, and numbered the people, and went up, he and the elders of Israel, before the people to Ai. And all the people, even the people of war that were with him, went up, and drew nigh, and came before the city, and pitched on the north side of Ai: now there was a valley between them and Ai. And he took about five thousand men, and set them to lie in ambush between Bethel and Ai, on the west side of the city. And when they had set the people, even all the host that was on the north of the city, and their liers in wait on the west of the city, Joshua went that night into the midst of the valley. And it came to pass, when the king of Ai saw it, that they hasted and rose up early, and the men of the city went out against Israel to battle, he and all his people, at a time appointed, before the plain; but he wist not that there were liers in ambush against him behind the city. And Joshua and all Israel made as if they were beaten before them, and fled by the way of the wilderness. And all the people that were in Ai were called together to pursue after them: and they pursued after Joshua, and were drawn away from the city. And there was not a man left in Ai or Bethel, that went not out after Israel: and they left the

city open, and pursued after Israel.

A believer must not pray a stereotyped prayer until the enemy has memorised the prayer points. He must be able to launch a surprise attack to deflect the enemy's arrows.

Prayer Points

1. **I will not carry any evil load in my life, in Jesus' name.**
2. **Lord, drain out satanic deposits from my business and handiwork.**
3. **Let all the strange hands and legs walk out of my business and handiwork, in the name of Jesus.**
4. **Let the spirit of favour fall upon me now, in the name of Jesus.**
5. **Lord, enlarge my coast.**
6. **I rebuke every devourer in my handiwork, in the name of Jesus.**
7. **Lord, cause ministering angels to bring in customers and money into my business.**
8. **I bind every spirit of error, in the name of Jesus.**
9. **Let every trouble emanating from envious business partners be rendered null and void, in the name of Jesus.**
10. **Lord surprise me with abundance in every area of my life.**
11. **I command a quit notice to (pick from the underlisted) . . . , in the name of Jesus.**
    - **evil legs on my finance**
    - **evil powers keeping the copy of my registration certificates.**
    - **every operational curse.**
12. **Let the anointing for money-yielding ideas fall upon my life, in the name of Jesus.**
13. **I bind every spirit of fake and useless investment, in Jesus' name.**
14. **I command every effect of strange money on my business to be neutralised, in the name of Jesus.**

15. Father Lord, let all satanic hosts against my prosperity receive blindness and commotion, in the name of Jesus.
16. All hindrances to my prosperity, be electrocuted, in Jesus' name.
17. Let all my mistakes be converted to miracles and testimonies, in the name of Jesus.

RULE NUMBER 18 - THE SMALL RARELY DEFEATS THE LARGE, THE WEAK RARELY DEFEATS THE STRONG

Pro 24:10 says:

If thou faint in the day of adversity, thy strength is small.

When your strength is small you are susceptible to defeat and when you are weak in the days of adversity you will be defeated. You must double your strength daily and surpass that of your enemy

Prayer Points

1. The enemy will not convert my destiny to rag in Jesus' name.
2. Lord, lay Your hands of fire and change upon my destiny.
3. I reject and renounce destiny –demoting names and nullify their evil effects upon my destiny, 'in Jesus' name.
4. Any evil record against my destiny in the heavenlies as a result of destiny-demoting names, be wiped off by the blood of Jesus.
5. I refuse to operate below my divine destiny, in Jesus' name.
6. Every power contending with my divine destiny, scatter, in the name of Jesus.
7. Lord, change my destiny to the best that will dumbfound my enemies.
8. Satan, I resist and rebuke your efforts to change my destiny, in the name of Jesus.
9. Satan, I remove from you the right to rob me of my divine destiny, in the name of Jesus.

10. I command all powers of darkness assigned to my destiny to leave and never to return, in the name of Jesus.
11. The desire of my enemy against my destiny will not be granted in the heavenlies, in the name of Jesus.
12. The designs of my enemy against my destiny shall be destroyed, in the name of Jesus.
13. The deposits of my enemies in the heavenlies against my destiny shall be destroyed, in the name of Jesus.
14. The destiny of my enemy shall not be my lot, in Jesus' name.
15. Whether Satan likes it or not, I awake to my destiny by fire, in the name of Jesus.
16. O Lord, give me new eyes to see into my destiny, in Jesus' name.
17. Conspiracy of darkness against my destiny, scatter by fire, in the name of Jesus.
18. The fire of the enemy against my destiny shall backfire, in Jesus' name.
19. No weapon formed against my destiny shall prosper, in Jesus' name.
20. You evil strongman attached to my destiny, be bound, in Jesus' name.
21. Every programme of failure fashioned against my destiny, die, in the name of Jesus.

RULE NUMBER 19 - KNOWING HOW TO WIN DOES NOT MEAN THAT YOU WILL WIN

James 1:22-25 says:

But be ye doers of the word, and not hearers only, deceiving your own selves. For if any be a hearer of the word, and not a doer, he is like unto a man beholding his natural face in a glass: For he beholdeth himself, and goeth his way, and straightway forgetteth what manner of man he was. But whoso looketh into the perfect law of liberty, and continueth therein, he being not a forgetful hearer, but a doer of the work, this man shall be blessed in his deed.

Knowing how to win does not mean you will win. Practising how to win is the step towards winning. The fact that you know all the names of soaps and detergents do not mean that you will be clean. Applying the soap is what matter.

Prayer Points

1. In this battle, I shall fight and win; I shall be a victor and not a victim, in the name of Jesus.
2. I put on the helmet of salvation, the belt of truth, the breastplate of righteousness. I wear the shoe of the gospel and I take the shield of faith as I go into this territorial intercession and warfare, in the name of Jesus.
3. I bind and rebuke the princes and powers in charge of this (mention the name of the city), in the name of Jesus
4. I command the fire of God on all the idols, traditions, sacrifices and rituals on this land, in the name of Jesus.
5. I break all the agreements made between the people of this city and satan, in the name of Jesus.
6. I decide and claim this city for God, in the name of Jesus.
7. Let the presence, dominion, authority and blessings of God be experienced in this city, in the name of Jesus.

VICTORY NUGGET

When God opens your eyes and gives you uncommon insight into obtaining unchallengeable victory, you will be blessed with the priviledge of sweatless victory. There are a few rules to focus attention on in this brief but insightful chapter.

RULE NUMBER 20 - VICTORY GOES TO THE HARDEST OR THE MEANEST

Exodus 22:18 says:

Thou shalt not suffer a witch to live.

Isaiah 9:4-5 says:

For thou hast broken the yoke of his burden, and the staff of his shoulder, the rod of his oppressor, as in the day of Midian. For every battle of the warrior is with confused noise, and garments rolled in blood; but this shall be with burning and fuel of fire.

This implies that in spiritual warfare, you need not be merciful or kind. You are wrestling against terrible powers and the victory goes to the meanest fighter. It is like a wrestling match where you can do anything to win.

Prayer Points

1. Let every satanic attack against my life in my dreams be converted to victory, in the name of Jesus.
2. Let all rivers, trees, forests, evil companions, evil pursuers, pictures of dead relatives, snakes, spirit husbands, spirit wives, masquerades manipulated against me in the dream, be completely destroyed by the power in the blood of the Lord Jesus.
3. I command every evil plantation in my life, come out with your roots in the name of Jesus! (Lay your hands on your stomach and keep repeating the emphasised area.)
4. Evil strangers in my body, come all the way out of your hiding places, in the name of Jesus.
5. I disconnect any conscious or unconscious linkage with demonic caterers, in the name of Jesus.
6. Let all avenues of eating or drinking spiritual poisons be closed, in the name of Jesus.
7. I cough out and vomit any food eaten from the table of the devil, in the name of Jesus. (Cough them out and vomit them in faith. Prime the expulsion.)
8. Let all negative materials circulating in my blood stream be evacuated, in the name of Jesus
9. I drink the blood of Jesus. (Physically swallow and drink it in faith. Keep doing this for some time.)
10. (Lay one hand on your head and the other on your stomach or navel and begin to pray like this:) Holy Ghost fire, burn from the top of my head to the sole of my feet. (Mention every organ of your body: your kidney, liver, intestines, blood, etc. You must not rush at this level, because the fire will actually come and you may start feeling the heat.)
11. I cut myself off from every spirit of... (mention the name of your place of birth), in the name of Jesus.
12. I cut myself off from every tribal spirit and curses, in the name of Jesus.

13. I cut myself off from every territorial spirit and curses, in the name of Jesus.
14. Holy Ghost fire, purge my life.

RULE NUMBER 21 - DEFENSIVE TACTICS ARE DIFFERENT FROM OFFENSIVE TACTICS

Eph 6:13 says:

Wherefore take unto you the whole armour of God, that ye may be able to withstand in the evil day, and having done all, to stand.

This rule of war is very important and must be well understand by the believer.

Prayer Points

1. I put on God's armour to resist the devil's tactics, in Jesus' name.
2. Lord, reveal to me any way that satan has a hold on my life.
3. I claim back any territory of my life handed over to satan, in the name of Jesus.
4. I bind all forces of evil in the air, fire, water and ground being set in motion against my life, in the name of Jesus.
5. I forbid any spirit from any source from harming me in any way, in the name of Jesus.
6. I reject every spirit of seduction, in the name of Jesus.
7. I refuse to let sin have dominion over me, in Jesus' name.
8. I reject every satanic promise on any department of my life, in the name of Jesus.
9. Let the powers setting themselves up in opposition to me be paralysed, in the name of Jesus.
10. I cancel the effect of all former satanic benefits in my life, in the name of Jesus.
11. I bind you spirit of anger in my life, in the name of Jesus.

12. Lord, fill me with strength to replace weakness.
13. Let all spiritual contamination be washed away by the blood of Jesus.
14. Let the cleansing and healing waters of the Lord flow into my life now, in the name of Jesus.

RULE NUMBER 22 - KEEP YOUR ENEMIES CONFUSED

Isaiah 9:5 says:

For every battle of the warrior is with confused noise, and garments rolled in blood; but this shall be with burning and fuel of fire.

Keep your enemies confused about the roots of your attack. This creates an advantage for you

Prayer Points

1. God, smite my enemies by the cheekbones, in Jesus' name.
2. My Father, break the teeth of the ungodly, in Jesus' name.
3. God, visit every power lying against me with destruction, in the name of Jesus.
4. Let my enemies fall by their own counsel, in the name of Jesus.
5. Lord, cast out my enemies in the multitude of their transgressions, in the name of Jesus.
6. Every organised worker of iniquity, depart from me, in the name of Jesus.
7. Let all my enemies be ashamed and sore vexed, in Jesus' name.
8. Let sudden shame be the lot of all my oppressors, in Jesus' name.
9. Every power planning to tear my soul like a lion, be dismantled, in the name of Jesus.
10. Let the wickedness of the wicked come to an end, O Lord, in the name of Jesus..
11. God, prepare the instruments of death against my enemies, in the name of .Jesus.

12. God, ordain Your arrows against my persecutors, in the name of Jesus.
13. Let every pit dug by the enemy become a grave for him, in the name of Jesus.
14. I render null and void the effect of any interaction with satanic agents moving around as men, in the name of Jesus.
15. I pull down the stronghold of evil strangers in every area of my life, in the name of Jesus.
16. Any negative transaction currently affecting my life negatively, be cancelled, in the name of Jesus.
17. I command all the dark works done against me in secret to be exposed and nullified, in the name of Jesus.
18. I loose myself from the bondage of any dark spirit, in the name of Jesus.
19. Let all incantations against me be cancelled, in the name of Jesus.
20. I command all oppressors to retreat and flee in defeat, in the name of Jesus
21. I bind every strongman having my goods in his possession, in the name of Jesus.
22. I break the curse of automatic failure working upon my life, in the name of Jesus.
23. Let the anointing to prosper fall mightily upon me now, in the name of Jesus.

RULE NUMBER 23 - SEEK ADEQUATE SPIRITUAL KNOWLEDGE

Psalm 144:1-2 says:

Blessed be the LORD my strength, which teacheth my hands to war, and my fingers to fight: My goodness, and my fortress; my high tower, and my deliverer; my shield, and he in whom I trust; who subdueth my people under me.

Seek adequate spiritual warfare knowledge. Do not go into war without any knowledge of how to fight.

Prayer Points

1. Let me be filled with the knowledge of His will, in Jesus' name.
2. Let me be filled with all wisdom and spiritual understanding, in the name of Jesus.
3. Father Lord, help me to work worthy of and pleasing to you, in the name of Jesus.
4. Father Lord, make me fruitful in every good work, in Jesus' name.
5. Lord, increase me in the knowledge of You.
6. Lord, strengthen me mightily.
7. Father Lord, let me be filled with the spirit of wisdom and understanding in the knowledge of Christ, in the name of Jesus.
8. Father Lord, let the eyes of my understanding be enlightened, in the name of Jesus.
9. Father Lord, let me be strengthened with might by Your spirit in the inner man, in the name of Jesus.
10. Father Lord, let Christ dwell in my heart by faith, in Jesus' name.
11. Father Lord, let me be rooted and grounded in love, in Jesus' name.
12. Lord, let me be filled with all fullness of You.
13. God, help me to comprehend the breadth, length, depth and height of the love of Christ, in the name of Jesus
14. Let the word of the Lord have free course and be glorified in me, in the name of Jesus.
15. Let the Lord of Peace give me peace in all areas of my life, in the name of Jesus.
16. Let utterance be given unto me to make known the mystery of the gospel, in the name of Jesus.
17. Lord, perfect what is lacking in my faith.
18. Lord, perfect Your good work in me.

RULE NUMBER 24 - DO NOT ABANDON THE INITIATIVE TO THE ENEMY

I Sam 17:45-49 says:

Then said David to the Philistine, Thou comest to me with a sword, and with a spear, and with a shield: but I come to thee in the name of the LORD of hosts, the God of the armies of Israel, whom thou hast defied. This day will the LORD deliver thee into mine hand; and I will smite thee, and take thine head from thee; and I will give the carcases of the host of the Philistines this day unto the fowls of the air, and to the wild beasts of the earth; that all the earth may know that there is a God in Israel. And all this assembly shall know that the LORD saveth not with sword and spear: for the battle is the LORD'S, and he will give you into our hands. And it came to pass, when the Philistine arose, and came and drew nigh to meet David, that David hasted, and ran toward the army to meet the Philistine. And David put his hand in his bag, and took thence a stone, and slang it, and smote the Philistine in his forehead, that the stone sunk into his forehead; and he fell upon his face to the earth.

You must take the initiative and lure the enemy to the battle front. In the case of Goliath and David, Goliath was surprised that David challenged him and he promised to waste David. David ran towards him, which implies that David started the war. That would have caused Goliath terrible fears because he was never used to people running toward him. He was used to people running away from him. I prophesy that you shall run towards your Goliath and destroy him, in the name of Jesus.

Prayer Points

1. I release myself from every ancestral demonic pollution, in the name of Jesus.
2. I release myself from every demonic pollution emanating from my parents' religion, in the name of Jesus.
3. I release myself from demonic pollution emanating from my past involvement in any demonic religion, in the name of Jesus.

4. I break and loose myself from every idol-related association, in the name of Jesus.
5. I release myself from every dream pollution, in Jesus' name.
6. Let every satanic attack against my life in my dreams be converted to victory, in the name of Jesus.
7. Let all rivers, trees, forests, evil companions, evil pursuers, pictures of dead relatives, snakes, spirit husbands, spirit wives and masquerades manipulated against me in the dream be completely destroyed by the power in the blood of the Lord Jesus.
8. I command every evil plantation in my life, come out with all your roots, in the name of Jesus! (Lay your hands on your stomach and keep repeating the emphasized area.)
9. Evil strangers in my body, come out of your hiding places, in the name of Jesus.
10. I disconnect any conscious or unconscious linkage with demonic caterers, in the name of Jesus.
11. Let all avenues of eating or drinking spiritual poisons be closed, in the name of Jesus.
12. I cough out and vomit any food eaten from the table of the devil, in the name of Jesus. (Cough them out and vomit them by faith. Prime the expulsion.)
13. Let all negative materials circulating in my blood stream be evacuated, in the name of Jesus.
14. I drink the blood of Jesus. (Physically swallow and drink it by faith. Keep doing this for some time.)
15. (Lay one hand on your head and the other on your stomach or navel and pray like this:) Holy Ghost fire, burn from the top of my head to the soles of my feet. (Mention every organ of your body: your kidney, liver, intestine, blood, etc. You must not rush at this level, because the fire will actually come and you may start feeling the heat.)
16. I cut myself off from every spirit of... (mention the name of your place of

birth), in the name of Jesus.

RULE NUMBER 25 -STARVE YOUR ENEMY

Romans 14:23 says:

And he that doubteth is damned if he eat, because he eateth not of faith: for whatsoever is not of faith is sin.

One thing that you need to really starve in your life is doubt. Once you feed your doubt, you are indirectly feeding your enemies. You must starve your enemies, else they become stronger and defeat you.

Prayer Points

1. Let all stubborn demons be starved to death, in Jesus' name.
2. I reject every evil peace in any department of my life, in the name of Jesus.
3. I seize power from every wicked spirit militating against my life, in the name of Jesus.
4. Lord, open my eyes and let me have a vision of Christ in this programme.
5. Lord, clean away from my life all that does not reflect You.
6. Holy Spirit, deposit Your wonders in my life in this programme, in the name of Jesus.
7. Holy Ghost, fill me that I can bring forth good fruit, in the name of Jesus.
8. Let the healing power of the Holy Spirit fall on me now, in the name Jesus.
9. I use the blood of Jesus to defy every satanic power fashioned against any department of my life, in the name of Jesus.
10. I put every evil hindrance to my breakthrough under my feet now, in the name of Jesus.
11. From the north, east and west, I claim all my blessings now, in the name of Jesus.
12. I receive all that God has for me in this programme, in the name of Jesus

13. I render every aggressive altar impotent, in the name of Jesus.

14. Every evil altar erected against me, be disgraced, in Jesus' name.

15. Anything done against my life under demonic anointing, be nullified, in the name of Jesus.

PRAYING TO CONFUSE THE ENEMY

This chapter focuses attention on important principles that will enable you to lead the enemy to a point of confusion. To scare the enemy and obtain unchallengeable victory, you need to pay attention to the following rules.

RULE NUMBER 26 - YOUR ENEMY MUST FIND YOU UNPREDICTABLE

John 3:8 says:

The wind bloweth where it listeth, and thou hearest the sound thereof, but canst not tell whence it cometh, and whither it goeth: so is every one that is born of the Spirit.

The enemies must find you mysteriously unpredictable. They should not know the kind of prayer you would pray, the kind of song you would sing and from where exactly you are going to launch your attack.

Prayer Points

1. Lord, give me understanding wisdom.
2. Angels of the living God, encamp round about me now and go before me to the competition, in the name of Jesus.

3. Father Lord, anoint my handiwork for success, in Jesus' name.
4. I claim divine wisdom to answer any questions directed at me in the competition, in the name of Jesus.
5. I excel my colleagues 10 times like Daniel, in Jesus' name
6. I will find favour before the panel, in the name of Jesus.
7. O Lord, perfect everything concerning my preparation for the competition. .
8. I bind .and render to nothing every spirit of fear, in Jesus' name.
9. I release myself from every of confusion and error, in the name of Jesus:
10. Father Lord, lay Your hand of fire upon my memory and give me retentive memory, in the name of Jesus.
11. Lord, keep me diligent in my private preparations.
12. Father, I dedicate all my faculties to you, in the name of Jesus.
13. Let all satanic mechanisms aimed at changing my destiny be frustrated, in the name of Jesus.
14. Let all unprofitable broadcasters of my goodness be silenced, in the name of Jesus.
15. Let every blessing confiscated by witchcraft spirits be released, in the name of Jesus.
16. Let every blessing confiscated by familiar spirits be released, in the name of Jesus.
17. Let every blessing confiscated by ancestral spirits be released, in the name of Jesus.
18. Let every blessing confiscated by envious enemies be released, in the name of Jesus.
19. Let every blessing confiscated by satanic agents be released, in the name of Jesus. .
20. Let every blessing confiscated by principalities be released, in the name of Jesus.
21. Let every blessing confiscated by rulers of darkness be released, in the

name of Jesus.

22. Let every blessing confiscated by evil powers be released, in the name of Jesus.
23. Let every blessing confiscated by spiritual wickedness in the heavenly places be released, in the name of Jesus.
24. Let all demonic reverse gears installed to hinder my progress be roasted, in the name of Jesus.
25. Anointing of the overcomer, fall upon me, in the name of Jesus.
26. I claim my divine promotion today, in the name of Jesus.
27. Thank God for answers to your prayer.

RULE NUMBER 27 - UTILISE THE HOURS OF THE NIGHT

Acts 16:25-26 says:

And at midnight Paul and Silas prayed, and sang praises unto God: and the prisoners heard them. And suddenly there was a great earthquake, so that the foundations of the prison were shaken: and immediately all the doors were opened, and every one's bands were loosed.

Job 34:20 says:

In a moment shall they die, and the people shall be troubled at midnight, and pass away: and the mighty shall be taken away without hand.

Judges 16:3 says:

And Samson lay till midnight, and arose at midnight, and took the doors of the gate of the city, and the two posts, and went away with them, bar and all, and put them upon his shoulders, and carried them up to the top of an hill that is before Hebron.

The mid-night is a period of spiritual transaction. It is a time for spiritual warfare. It is the best time to challenge the enemy because he will be sleeping and unprepared. There was a case of a woman who was constantly facing demonic attacks. I gave her some prayer points and as she began to pray a large, dark cat wanted to escape through the window. As she forcefully closed the window the cat's leg was cut off. By the time she got to the office the next day the assistant matron had been rushed to the hospital. Some unexplainable thing had cut off her legs.

Prayer Points

1. Every terror of the night, scatter, in the name of Jesus.
2. Every witchcraft challenge of my destiny, die, in Jesus' name.
3. Every seed of the enemy in my destiny, die, in Jesus' name.
4. Every dream of demotion, die, in the name of Jesus.
5. Power of God, uproot wicked plantations from my life, in the name of Jesus.
6. Every destiny vulture, vomit my breakthroughs, in the name of Jesus.
7. Every evil power that pursued my parents, release me, in the name of Jesus.
8. I fire back every witchcraft arrow fired into my life as a baby, in the name of Jesus.
9. Fire of God, thunder of God, purse my pursuers, in the name of Jesus.
10. Holy Ghost fire, purge my blood from satanic injection, in the name of Jesus.
11. Every evil power of my father's house that will not let me go, die, in the name of Jesus.
12. Every power designed to spoil my life, scatter, in the name of Jesus.
13. Every herbal power working against my destiny, die, in the name of Jesus.
14. I kill every sickness in my life, in the name of Jesus.
15. Every power of the idols of my father's house, die, in the name of Jesus.
16. Every evil power pursuing me from my father's house, die, in the name of Jesus.
17. Every evil power pursuing me from my mother's house, die, in the name

of Jesus.

18. Every witchcraft tree binding my placenta, die, in the name of Jesus.
19. Where is the Lord God of Elijah? Arise and fight for me, in the name of Jesus.
20. Every destiny-demoting dream, scatter, in the name of Jesus.

RULE NUMBER 28 - ENSURE THAT THE PRINCE OF THIS WORLD HAS NOTHING IN YOU

John 14:30 says:

Hereafter I will not talk much with you: for the prince of this world cometh, and hath nothing in me.

The devil has a very powerful x-ray machine to detect his attributes in anyone. You must be sure that nothing of the prince of this world is in you because those things will invite him and make you a weak warrior.

Prayer Points

1. I shall excel this day and nothing shall defile me, in the name of Jesus.
2. I shall possess the gates of my enemies, in the name of Jesus.
3. The Lord shall anoint me with the oil of gladness above others, in the name of Jesus.
4. The fire of the enemy shall not burn me, in the name of Jesus.
5. My ears shall hear good news, I shall not hear the voice of the enemy, in the name of Jesus.
6. My future is secured in Christ, in the name of Jesus.
7. My God has created me to do certain definite services. He has committed to my hands some assignments which He has not committed to anyone else. He has not created me for nothing. I shall do good. I shall do His work. I shall be an agent of peace. I will trust Him in whatever I do and wherever I am. I can never be thrown away or downgraded, in the name

of Jesus.

8. There will be no poverty of body, soul and spirit in my life, in the name of Jesus.

9. The anointing of God upon my life gives me favour in His eyes and in the eyes of men all the days of my life, in Jesus' name.

10. I shall not labour in vain, in the name of Jesus.

11. I shall walk everyday in victory and liberty of the spirit, in the name of Jesus.

12. I receive the mouth and wisdom which my adversaries are not able to resist, in Jesus' name.

13. Let every battle in the heavenlies be won in favour of the angels conveying my blessings today, in Jesus' name.

RULE NUMBER 29 - LEARN HOW TO ADAPT QUICKLY TO CHANGES IN CIRCUMSTANCES

Judges 16:1-21 says:

Then went Samson to Gaza, and saw there an harlot, and went in unto her. And it was told the Gazites, saying, Samson is come hither. And they compassed him in, and laid wait for him all night in the gate of the city, and were quiet all the night, saying, In the morning, when it is day, we shall kill him. And Samson lay till midnight, and arose at midnight, and took the doors of the gate of the city, and the two posts, and went away with them, bar and all, and put them upon his shoulders, and carried them up to the top of an hill that is before Hebron. And it came to pass afterward, that he loved a woman in the valley of Sorek, whose name was Delilah. And the lords of the Philistines came up unto her, and said unto her, Entice him, and see wherein his great strength lieth, and by what means we may prevail against him, that we may bind him to afflict him: and we will give thee every one of us eleven hundred pieces of silver. And Delilah said to Samson, Tell me, I pray thee, wherein thy great strength lieth, and wherewith thou mightest be bound to afflict thee. And Samson said unto her, If they bind me with seven green withs that were never dried, then shall I be weak, and be as another

man. Then the lords of the Philistines brought up to her seven green withs which had not been dried, and she bound him with them. Now there were men lying in wait, abiding with her in the chamber. And she said unto him, The Philistines be upon thee, Samson. And he brake the withs, as a thread of tow is broken when it toucheth the fire. So his strength was not known. And Delilah said unto Samson, Behold, thou hast mocked me, and told me lies: now tell me, I pray thee, wherewith thou mightest be bound. And he said unto her, If they bind me fast with new ropes that never were occupied, then shall I be weak, and be as another man. Delilah therefore took new ropes, and bound him therewith, and said unto him, The Philistines be upon thee, Samson. And there were liers in wait abiding in the chamber. And he brake them from off his arms like a thread. And Delilah said unto Samson, Hitherto thou hast mocked me, and told me lies: tell me wherewith thou mightest be bound. And he said unto her, If thou weavest the seven locks of my head with the web. And she fastened it with the pin, and said unto him, The Philistines be upon thee, Samson. And he awaked out of his sleep, and went away with the pin of the beam, and with the web. And she said made him sleep upon her knees; and she called for a man, and she caused him to shave off the seven locks of his head; and she began to afflict him, and his strength went from him. And she said, The Philistines be upon thee, Samson. And he awoke out of his sleep, and said, I will go out as at other times before, and shake myself. And he wist not that the LORD was departed from him. But the Philistines took him, and put out his eyes, and brought him down to Gaza, and bound him with fetters of brass; and he did grind in the prison house.

This was the mistake of Samson. He could not adapt to the changes in circumstances. By the time Delilah came, Samson did not know that the battle strategies had changed and that the Philistines were no longer interested in hand-to-hand battle with him. They had devised a new strategy.

Prayer Points

1. O Lord, as I experience biological and emotional changes, let Your joy be my strength, in the name of Jesus.

2. Father, be glorified in my life, in the name of Jesus.
3. God, arise according to Jeremiah 29: 11 and give me expected end of safety and joy, in Jesus' name.
4. I shield myself inside the envelope of divine fire away from evil observers and evil monitors, in Jesus' name.
5. God, give me heavenly care and proper development for my baby, in the name of Jesus.
6. God, direct me throughout this process of pregnancy, in the name of Jesus.
7. By Your mercy, O God, deliver me and my babies from any harvest of the seeds of iniquity sown in the past, in the name of Jesus.
8. God, let my case stand out for dumbfounding success, in the name of Jesus.
9. You who cause me to conceive, cause me to bring forth, in the name of Jesus (Isa. 66:9).
10. All things must work together for my good, in the name of Jesus.
11. I bind every spirit of error, in the name of Jesus.
12. As a spiritual child of Abraham, I am fruitful and will multiply, in the name. of Jesus.
13. My pregnancy shall be firmly established and shall not miscarry before the normal delivery time, in the name of Jesus.
14. My children shall serve God's purpose for me to multiply and subdue the earth, in the name of Jesus.
15. God, deliver me from morning sickness and any complication, in the name of Jesus.
16. I stand against any birth defects in my babies and claim perfection for them, in the name of Jesus.

RULE NUMBER 30 - VARY YOUR TACTICS WHEN NECESSARY

Joshua 8:1-26 says:

And the LORD said unto Joshua, Fear not, neither be thou dismayed: take all the people of war with thee, and arise, go up to Ai: see, I have given into thy hand the king of Ai, and his people, and his city, and his land: And thou shalt do to Ai and her king as thou didst unto Jericho and her king: only the spoil thereof, and the cattle thereof, shall ye take for a prey unto yourselves: lay thee an ambush for the city behind it. So Joshua arose, and all the people of war, to go up against Ai: and Joshua chose out thirty thousand mighty men of valour, and sent them away by night. And he commanded them, saying, Behold, ye shall lie in wait against the city, even behind the city: go not very far from the city, but be ye all ready: And I, and all the people that are with me, will approach unto the city: and it shall come to pass, when they come out against us, as at the first, that we will flee before them, (For they will come out after us) till we have drawn them from the city; for they will say, They flee before us, as at the first: therefore we will flee before them. Then ye shall rise up from the ambush, and seize upon the city: for the LORD your God will deliver it into your hand. And it shall be, when ye have taken the city, that ye shall set the city on fire: according to the commandment of the LORD shall ye do. See, I have commanded you. Joshua therefore sent them forth: and they went to lie in ambush, and abode between Bethel and Ai, on the west side of Ai: but Joshua lodged that night among the people. And Joshua rose up early in the morning, and numbered the people, and went up, he and the elders of Israel, before the people to Ai. And all the people, even the people of war that were with him, went up, and drew nigh, and came before the city, and pitched on the north side of Ai: now there was a valley between them and Ai. And he took about five thousand men, and set them to lie in ambush between Bethel and Ai, on the west side of the city. And when they had set the people, even all the host that was on the north of the city, and their liers in wait on the west of the city, Joshua went that night into the midst of the valley. And it came to pass, when the king of Ai saw it, that they hasted and rose up early, and the men of the city went out against Israel to battle, he and all his people, at a time appointed, before the plain; but he wist not that there were liers in ambush against him behind the city. And Joshua and all Israel made as if they were beaten before them, and fled by the way of the wilderness. And all the people that were in Ai were called together to pursue after them: and they pursued after Joshua, and were drawn away from the city. And there was not a man left in Ai or Bethel, that went not out after Israel: and they left the city open, and pursued after Israel. And the LORD said unto Joshua, Stretch out the spear that is in thy hand toward Ai; for I will give it into thine hand. And Joshua stretched out the spear that he had in his hand toward the city. And the ambush arose quickly out of their place, and they ran as soon as he had stretched out his hand: and they entered into the city, and took it, and hasted and set the city on fire. And when the men of Ai looked behind them, they saw, and, behold, the smoke of the city ascended up to heaven, and they had no power to flee this way or that way: and the people that fled to the wilderness turned back upon the pursuers. And when Joshua and all Israel saw that the ambush had taken the city, and that the smoke of the city ascended, then they turned again, and slew the men of Ai. And the other issued out of the city against them; so they were in the midst of Israel, some on this side, and some on that side: and they smote them, so that they let none of them remain or escape. And the king of Ai they took alive, and brought him to Joshua. And it came to pass, when Israel had made an end of slaying all the inhabitants of Ai in the field, in the wilderness wherein they chased them, and when they were all fallen on the edge of the sword, until they were consumed, that all the Israelites returned unto Ai, and smote it with the edge of the sword. And so it was, that all that fell that day, both of men and women, were twelve thousand, even all the men of Ai. For Joshua drew not his hand back, wherewith he stretched out the spear, until he had utterly destroyed all the inhabitants of Ai.

Do not fight like a robot. You must be able to vary your tactics.

Prayer Points

1. Every demonic instrument of oppression set aside to abort my pregnancy, break to pieces, in the name of Jesus.
2. Lord, fight against the destroyer working against my increase and

fruitfulness, in the name of Jesus.

3. Every demonic doctor or nurse delegated by satan to destroy my pregnancy, inject yourself to death, in Jesus' name.
4. Let the blood of Jesus wash me and show me mercy, in the name of Jesus.
5. Every evil remote controlling gadget being used to manipulate my pregnancy, be roasted by fire, in Jesus' name.
6. Thou Man of war, save me out of the hands of the wicked midwives, in the name of Jesus.
7. I render every weapon fashioned against my pregnancy impotent, in the name of Jesus.
8. Lord, overthrow every Egyptian working against me in the midst of the sea, in the name of Jesus.
9. I close down every satanic broadcasting station fashioned against my pregnancy, in the name of Jesus.
10. I will see the great work of the Lord as I am delivered of my children safely, in the name of Jesus.
11. I refuse to harbour any pregnancy killer in any department of my life, in the name of Jesus.
12. Every horse and the rider in my womb, family or office, be thrown into the sea of forgetfulness, in the name of Jesus.
13. I bind every spirit of error assigned against my pregnancy, in the name of Jesus:
14. Lord, send Your light before me to drive miscarriage away from my womb and life, in the name of Jesus.

RULE NUMBER 31 - WORRY WILL LEAD TO BLUNDERS AND STRENGTHEN THE ENEMY

John 14:1 says:

Let not your heart be troubled: ye believe in God, believe also in me.

John 14:27 says:

Peace I leave with you, my peace I give unto you: not as the world giveth, give I unto you. Let not your heart be troubled, neither let it be afraid.

The Bible commands that you should not let your heart be troubled but to believe in God. When you are worried, anxious and confused, you are indirectly giving the enemy a clear advantage to defeat you.

Prayer Points

1. I receive strength and power to be a warrior and not to worry, in the name of Jesus.
2. I smash the head of the strongman on the wall of fire, in the name of Jesus.
3. Let hell open its mouth without measure and swallow all suckers of peace in my life, in the name of Jesus.
4. There shall be no regrouping and no reinforcement against me by the strongmen in my family, in the name of Jesus.
5. Let the angels of God roll the stones of fire to hinder the strongman on my ways, in the name of Jesus.
6. I cause open disgrace to all strongmen in my family, in Jesus name.
7. Let all the enemies of my soul start their days in confusion and end it in destruction, in the name of Jesus.
8. Lord, release from my mind from any image of jealousy, lust and evil intention.
9. I stand against all confusing forces within me, in Jesus' name.
10. Lord, order my inner life so that I can hear You.
11. Lord, let me see what You see in me.
12. Lord, make me uncomfortable till I get to the right track.
13. Lord, wash my brain with the blood of Jesus and remove bad habits which are physically engraved there.
14. Lord, heal any hormonal imbalance or other harmful secretions in my body.

15. Lord, heal me in whatever needs to be healed.
16. Lord, replace in me whatever needs to be replaced.
17. Lord, transform me in whatever needs to be transformed.

RULE NUMBER 32 - YOU MUST BE DISCIPLINED

1 Tim 1:18-19 says:

This charge I commit unto thee, son Timothy, according to the prophecies which went before on thee, that thou by them mightest war a good warfare; Holding faith, and a good conscience; which some having put away concerning faith have made shipwreck.

Believers must be disciplined in the way they live their lives. Some people eat anything without self-control. They buy food anywhere and eat anywhere without discrimination and limitation. This could lead to being poisoned or being infected. Discipline is a spiritual weapon.

Prayer Points

1. I nullify all spiritual weapons being used to slow down my progress, in the name of Jesus.
2. I cancel all strongholds that the spirit of fear has built in me, in the name of Jesus.
3. Lord, begin to baptize every area of my life with your dumbfounding miracles.
4. I nullify every evil effect of fear in my life, in the name of Jesus.
5. Lord, give me the spirit of boldness.
6. Let all the powers that shake off God's blessings in my life be removed and be destroyed, in the name of Jesus.
7. I place myself under the Cross of Jesus.
8. I cover myself with the precious blood of Jesus.
9. I surround myself with the light of Christ.
10. The devil will not interfere with the Lord's work in my life, in the name

of Jesus.

11. I put on God's armour to resist the devil's tactics, in Jesus' name.

12. Lord, reveal to me any way that satan has a hold on my life.

13. I claim back any territory of my life handed to satan, in the name of Jesus.

14. I bind all forces of evil in the air, fire, water and ground being set in motion against my life, in the name of Jesus.

15. I forbid any spirit from any source from harming me in any way, in the name of Jesus.

16. I reject every spirit of seduction, in the name of Jesus.

17. I refuse to let sin have dominion over me, in the name of Jesus.

18. I reject every satanic promise on any department of my life, in the name of Jesus.

19. Let the powers setting themselves up in opposition to me be paralysed, in the name of Jesus.

20. I cancel the effect of all former satanic benefits in my life, in the name of Jesus.

21. I bind you spirit of anger in my life, in the name of Jesus.

22. Lord, fill me with strength to replace weakness.

23. Let all spiritual contamination be washed away by the blood of Jesus.

24. Let the cleansing and healing waters of the Lord flow into my life now, in the name of Jesus.

25. Father, I surrender to you today with all my heart and soul, in the name of Jesus.

26. Lord, come into my life in a deeper way.

27. I say yes to you today, O Lord.

BATTLE TACTICS

Going blindly into the arena of a battle will make you a loser. You must follow the following rules

RULE NUMBER 33 - YOU MUST KNOW YOUR BATTLE FIELD

Zech 14:14 says:

And Judah also shall fight at Jerusalem; and the wealth of all the heathen round about shall be gathered together, gold, and silver, and apparel, in great abundance.

When you are at war and you do not understand the battlefield, the enemy will waste you and disgrace you. You must understand your battlefield properly. In football matches, there is what is called "Home advantage." You must take advantage of your home, or prepare better if it is an away battle.

Prayer Points

1. I command my battle to change to blessing, in Jesus' name.
2. Let every mountain of satanic confrontation be disgraced, in the name of Jesus.

3. Let every mountain of impossibility be dashed to pieces, in the name of Jesus.
4. Let new wells spring up in my desert, in the name of Jesus.
5. Lord, bear me up on eagle's wings before my enemies.
6. Lord, anoint my eyes to see my divine opportunities.
7. I refuse to allow my present to influence my future negatively.
8. Let every satanic battle confronting me fall apart, in Jesus' name.
9. I throw down the strongman of financial embarrassment, in Jesus' name.
10. I declare myself free from the plagues of spiritual Egypt, in the name Jesus.
11. I command all crooked and difficult areas of my life to begin to yield testimonies, in the name Jesus.
12. Let the spirit of excellence manifest in every area of my life, in the name Jesus.
13. Let the fear of me fill the mind of the enemies and let them panic, in the name Jesus.
14. My year shall not be in struggle but in prosperity, in Jesus' name.
15. Let the oppressors drown in their own Red Sea, in Jesus' name.
16. I receive power to leap over every wall that the enemy has built, in the name of Jesus.
17. Let the enemy fall into his own trap, in the name of Jesus
18. Lord, make my miracle invisible to my enem ies.
19. Lord, re-organise my system to confuse evil observers.
20. I resist all spiritual sabotage and cunning attacks, in the name Jesus.
21. Let the fire of God protect my miracle, in the name Jesus.

RULE NUMBER 34 - STICK TO RESOURCES THAT STRENGTHEN YOU

Matt 17:20-21 says:

And Jesus said unto them, Because of your unbelief: for verily I say unto you, If ye have faith as a grain of mustard seed, ye shall say unto this mountain, Remove hence to yonder place; and it shall remove; and nothing shall be impossible unto you. Howbeit this kind goeth not out but by prayer and fasting.

Those things that you do that increase your spiritual power and strength, stick to them. It is a very important rule of spiritual warfare.

Prayer Points

1. Any power that has been supplying strength to problems in my life, be wasted, in the name of Jesus.
2. I refuse to swim in the ocean of problems, in the name of Jesus.
3. Every remotely controlled problem energised by household wickedness, be devoured by the Lion of Judah, in Jesus' name.
4. I sack and disband any power behind the problems of my life, in the name of Jesus.
5. Lord Jesus, I refuse to be kept busy by the devil.
6. I receive power to convert failures designed for my life to outstanding successes, in the name of Jesus.
7. I receive power to close down every satanic factory designed for me, in the name of Jesus.
8. Angels of blessings, begin to locate me now for my own blessing in this programme, in the name of Jesus.
9. Powers behind accidental problems, I am not your candidate. Fall down and die, in the name of Jesus.
10. I receive the power to break every circle of problems, in the name of Jesus.
11. Every attempt being made by destiny killers against my destiny, be

frustrated unto death, in the name of Jesus.

12. I command the fire of God to come upon destiny killers working against my destiny, in the name of Jesus.

13. I remove my destiny from the camp of destiny killers, in the name of Jesus.

14. I use the fire of God and the blood of Jesus to surround my destiny, in the name of Jesus.

15. Every power working against the fruitfulness of my destiny, be disgraced, in the name of Jesus

16. I command my destiny to reject every bewitchment, in the name of Jesus.

17. I deliver my destiny from the grip of destiny killers, in Jesus' name.

RULE NUMBER 35 - ALWAYS KEEP YOURSELF AT A POSITION THAT PUTS YOUR ENEMY AT A DISADVANTAGE

Neh. 4:1-6 says:

But it came to pass, that when Sanballat heard that we builded the wall, he was wroth, and took great indignation, and mocked the Jews. And he spake before his brethren and the army of Samaria, and said, What do these feeble Jews? will they fortify themselves? will they sacrifice? will they make an end in a day? will they revive the stones out of the heaps of the rubbish which are burned? Now Tobiah the Ammonite was by him, and he said, Even that which they build, if a fox go up, he shall even break down their stone wall. Hear, O our God; for we are despised: and turn their reproach upon their own head, and give them for a prey in the land of captivity: And cover not their iniquity, and let not their sin be blotted out from before thee: for they have provoked thee to anger before the builders. So built we the wall; and all the wall was joined together unto the half thereof: for the people had a mind to work.

The way you position yourself is very important. Do not position your body, spirit or soul in a way that gives the enemy an advantage. Be in the realm of victory.

Prayer Points

1. Every satanic barrier designed to hold me back from my desired position, be shattered to pieces, in Jesus' name.
2. Let every evil decree working against my potentials be revoked, in the name of Jesus.
3. I remove by fire every mark of poverty in my life, in the name of Jesus.
4. My life, my business, reject all marks of poverty, in Jesus name.
5. Every evil hand that canied me when I was a baby, roast by fire, in the name of Jesus.
6. You mountain of debt, programmed to put me into poverty, be cast away, in the name of Jesus.
7. I recover my placenta from the cage of wicked people, in the name of Jesus.
8. Every agent attached to profitlessness in my life, be paralysed, in the name of Jesus.
9. I receive divine direction, in the name of Jesus.
10. Lord, give me divine revelation.
11. Lord, let Your glory overshadow every work I do.
12. God arise, and disgrace every trap of poverty in my family, in the name of Jesus.
13. God arise, and scatter every trap of poverty in my life, in the name of Jesus
14. The labour of my hands shall prosper, in the name of Jesus.
15. Every waster of my prosperity, be impotent, in Jesus' name.
16. Every known and unknown opposer of my comfort, be paralysed, in the name of Jesus.
17. Anything planted in my life to disgrace me, come out with all your roots, in the name of Jesus.
18. I reject demonic stagnation of my blessing, in Jesus' name.
19. I reject weak financial breakthroughs. I claim big financial breakthroughs,

in the name of Jesus.

RULE NUMBER 36 - YOU MUST LEARN TO ASSESS THE STRENGTH OF YOUR ENEMY

2 Cor 2:9-11 says:

For to this end also did I write, that I might know the proof of you, whether ye be obedient in all things. To whom ye forgive any thing, I forgive also: for if I forgave any thing, to whom I forgave it, for your sakes forgave I it in the person of Christ; Lest Satan should get an advantage of us: for we are not ignorant of his devices.

For to this end also did I write, that I might know the proof of you, whether ye be obedient in all things. To whom ye forgive any thing, I forgive also: for if I forgave any thing, to whom I forgave it, for your sakes forgave I it in the person of Christ; Lest Satan should get an advantage of us: for we are not ignorant of his devices.

Here, your Bible reading, listening to the Holy Spirit and meditation play important roles.

Prayer Points

1. I release myself from every family pattern of poverty, in the name of Jesus.
2. I refuse to allow my wealth to die on any evil altar, in Jesus' name.
3. I reject every prosperity paralysis, in the name of Jesus.
4. I possess all my foreign benefits today, in Jesus' name.
5. My pocket will not leak, in the name of Jesus.
6. I dash every poverty dream to the ground, in Jesus' name.
7. Every good thing that my hands have started to build, they shall finish it, in the name of Jesus.
8. I refuse to become the foot-mat of amputators, in Jesus' name.
9. Let my helpers appear, let my hinderances disappear, in the name of

Jesus.

10. God of providence, raise divine capital for me, in Jesus' name.

11. I occupy my rightful position, in the name of Jesus.

12. Every delayed and denied prosperity, manifest by fire, in the name of Jesus.

13. Every bewitched account, receive deliverance, in Jesus' name.

14. Every snail anointing on my blessings, fall down and die, in the name of Jesus.

15. Every power broadcasting my goodness for evil, be silenced, in the name of Jesus.

16. I refuse to lock the doors of blessings against myself, in the name of Jesus.

17. I release myself from every spirit of poverty, in Jesus' name.

18. I curse the spirit of poverty with the curse of the Lord, in Jesus' name.

19. I release myself from every bondage of poverty, in Jesus' name.

20. The riches of the gentiles shall come to me, in Jesus' name.

21. Let divine magnets of prosperity be planted in my hands, in the name of Jesus.

22. I retrieve my purse from the hands of Judas, in Jesus' name.

RULE NUMBER 37 - UNDERSTAND THE STRATEGY OF RETREAT FROM BAD SITUATIONS

Mark 1:35 says:

And in the morning, rising up a great while before day, he went out, and departed into a solitary place, and there prayed.

You must know the best time to go a little bit aside and re-plan your strategies. There is a time to take cover and a time to take over. If you try to take over when you are supposed to take cover there will be problems.

Prayer Points

1. Lord, give unto me the eagle eye and the eyes of Elisha to foresee market situations.
2. Lord, give me wisdom to walk out of any unfavourable business situations.
3. Father, help me to formulate a plan of recovery to keep me at the top, in the name of Jesus.
4. Lord, send me divine counsellors who can help me with my business.
5. Lord, always help me to identify evil business traps.
6. Lord, help me to erect safeguards to prevent business failure.
7. Let Your seal and divine stamp fall upon all my business proposals, in the name of Jesus.
8. My proposals, be too hot for the enemy to sit upon, in Jesus' name.
9. Father, give me the anointing to get the job done above and beyond my own strength, abilities, gifts and talents.
10. Lord, help me to be on the right way to provide better products and services.
11. Lord, help me to yield to the Holy Spirit whenever I encounter circumstances beyond my knowledge.

RECIPE FOR ALL ROUND VICTORY

Total victory can only be achieved when you discover outstanding principles. So far we have discussed lots of powerful principles, we shall examine more principles in this chapter

RULE NUMBER 38 - QUENCH YOUR INTERNAL BATTLES

2 Sam 22:46 says:

Strangers shall fade away, and they shall be afraid out of their close places.

Psalm 18:45 says:

The strangers shall fade away, and be afraid out of their close places.

If battles are ragging within you and you have not quieted them by praising God, the word of God and or prayers, you will become a loser if you go for outside battles. Many people are looking for the enemy outside but in the real sense the real enemy is inside. The Bible says: "As soon as they hear of me, they shall obey me. Strangers shall surrender themselves to me. Stranger shall fade away and shall be afraid out of their close places." As you read this book,

I bind every internal stranger confusing you, in the name of Jesus.

Prayer Points

1. I shall walk everyday in victory and liberty of the spirit, in the name of Jesus.
2. I receive the mouth and wisdom which my adversaries are not able to resist, in Jesus' name.
3. Let every battle in the heavenlies be won in favour of the angels conveying my blessings today, in Jesus' name.
4. Lord, let the wicked be shaken out of my heavens, in the name of Jesus.
5. Sun, as you are coming out today, uproot every wickedness targeted against my life, in the name of Jesus.
6. I programme blessings into the sun for my life, in the name of Jesus.
7. Sun, I have risen before you, and I cancel every evil programme projected into you by wicked powers against my life, in the name of Jesus.
8. You this day, you will not destroy my prosperity, in the name of Jesus.
9. Sun, moon and stars, carry your afflictions back to the sender, and release them against him, in Jesus' name.
10. God, arise and uproot everything you have not planted in the heavenlies that is working against me, in Jesus' name.
11. Let the wicked be shaken out from the ends of the earth, in the name of Jesus.
12. Sun, as you come forth, uproot all the wickedness that has come against my life, in the name of Jesus.
13. I programme blessings into the sun, the moon and the stars for my life today, in the name of Jesus.

RULE NUMBER 39 - FIGHT COURAGEOUSLY AND DESPERATELY

Mark 10:46-52 says:

And they came to Jericho: and as he went out of Jericho with his disciples and a great number of people, blind Bartimaeus, the son of Timaeus, sat by the highway side begging. And when he heard that it was Jesus of Nazareth, he began to cry out, and say, Jesus, thou Son of David, have mercy on me. And many charged him that he should hold his peace: but he cried the more a great deal, Thou Son of David, have mercy on me. And Jesus stood still, and commanded him to be called. And they call the blind man, saying unto him, Be of good comfort, rise; he calleth thee. And he, casting away his garment, rose, and came to Jesus. And Jesus answered and said unto him, What wilt thou that I should do unto thee? The blind man said unto him, Lord, that I might receive my sight. And Jesus said unto him, Go thy way; thy faith hath made thee whole. And immediately he received his sight, and followed Jesus in the way.

There is a heavenly department for holy desperation. When desperation starts progress begin.

Prayer Points

1. Let the stars of heaven begin to fight for me, in the name of Jesus.
2. God, arise and scatter every conspiracy in the heavenlies that is against me. in the name of Jesus.
3. I break with the blood of Jesus all evil soul-ties affecting my life, in the name of Jesus.
4. Spirit of the living God, come upon my life and place a shield of protection around me, in the name of Jesus.
5. Every chain of inherited witchcraft in my family, break, in the name of Jesus.
6. Every ladder used by witchcraft against me, be roasted, in the name of Jesus.
7. Any door that I have opened to witchcraft in any area of my life, be closed forever by the blood of Jesus.

8. I revoke every witchcraft verdict on my life, in the name of Jesus.
9. I send confusion into the camp of household witchcraft, in the name of Jesus
10. Stubborn witchcraft, release me, in the name of Jesus.
11. Every witchcraft power working against my destiny, fall down and die, in the name of Jesus.
12. Every incantation, ritual and witchcraft power against my destiny, fall down and die, in the name of Jesus.
13. I break the power of the occult, witchcraft and familiar spirits over my life, in the name of Jesus.
14. Witchcraft opposition, receive the rain of affliction, in the name of Jesus.
15. I cancel every witchcraft verdict against my life, in the name of Jesus.
16. I command every arrow of witchcraft in my life: come out with all your roots in the name of Jesus! (Lay your hands on your stomach and pray aggressively).

RULE NUMBER 40 - WHEN THE BATTLE IS HARD KEEP PRESSING ON

Heb 12:3-4 says:

For consider him that endured such contradiction of sinners against himself, lest ye be wearied and faint in your minds. Ye have not yet resisted unto blood, striving against sin.

Never think of giving up. No matter how hard and seemingly difficult the battle might look, do not give up.

Prayer Points

1. Every yoke of hardship working against me, be broken, in the name of Jesus.
2. Every serpent and scorpion swallowing my benefits, vomit them and die, in the name of Jesus.
3. All my blessings imprisoned by the grave, come forth, in the name of

Jesus

4. I release my blessings from the hands of any dead relatives, in the name of Jesus.
5. I withdraw my blessings from the hands of all dead enemies, in the name of Jesus.
6. I disgrace every witchcraft burial, in the name of Jesus.
7. Just as the grave could not detain Jesus, no power can detain my miracles, in the name of Jesus.
8. That which hinders me from greatness, give way now, in the name of Jesus.
9. Whatsoever has been done against me using the ground, be neutralised, in the name of Jesus.
10. Every unfriendly friend, be exposed, in the name of Jesus.
11. Anything representing my image in the spirit world, I withdraw you, in the name of Jesus.
12. All the camps of my enemies, receive confusion, in the name of Jesus.
13. Lord, empower my life with Your authority, over every demonic force that set themselves against my life.

RULE NUMBER 41 - ALWAYS MOVE RAPIDLY AND MISS NO OPPORTUNITY

Eccl 11:1-6 says:

Cast thy bread upon the waters: for thou shalt find it after many days. Give a portion to seven, and also to eight; for thou knowest not what evil shall be upon the earth. If the clouds be full of rain, they empty themselves upon the earth: and if the tree fall toward the south, or toward the north, in the place where the tree falleth, there it shall be. He that observeth the wind shall not sow; and he that regardeth the clouds shall not reap. As thou knowest not what is the way of the spirit, nor how the bones do grow in the womb of her that is with child: even so thou knowest not the works of God who maketh all. In the morning sow thy seed, and in the evening withhold

not thine hand: for thou knowest not whether shall prosper, either this or that, or whether they both shall be alike good.

This is important because you can never tell when a jack-pot will fall for you from heaven. All facilities provided for you by the house of God must be dully utilised. Bible studies must be taken seriously. Revival meetings and prayer meetings must not be missed.

Prayer Points

1. I paralyse every satanic opportunity contending against my life, in the name of Jesus.
2. Every incantation, ritual and witchcraft power against my destiny, fall down and die, in the name of Jesus.
3. I render null and void the influence of destiny swallowers, in the name of Jesus.
4. Every household wickedness struggling to re-arrange my destiny, loose your hold, in the name of Jesus.
5. The rod of the wicked shall not rest upon my life, in Jesus' name.
6. I refuse to be removed from the divine agenda, in Jesus' name.
7. Holy Spirit, I invite You into my imagination, in Jesus' name.
8. Lord, bring to light every darkness shielding my potentials, in the name of Jesus.
9. I break every curse of backwardness, in the name of Jesus.
10. I recover myself from every evil diversion, in the name of Jesus.
11. I shall not come to the world in vain, in the name of Jesus.
12. Every forest and rock demon assigned against me, fall down and die, in the name of Jesus.
13. Every local charm made against me, be roasted, in the name of Jesus.
14. I release myself from ungodly parental linkage, in Jesus' name.
15. Lord Jesus, manifest Yourself in my life by Your name called 'Wonderful'.
16. Every bird of death assigned against me, fall down and die, in the name

of Jesus.

17. I withdraw the food and drink of my problems, in Jesus' name.

18. No evil family river shall flow into my life, in the name of Jesus.

19. I withdraw my progress from every satanic regulation and domination, in the name of Jesus.

RULE NUMBER 42 - ATTACK THE ENEMY'S COOPERATION AND COMMUNICATION

2 Cor 10:4-5 says:

(For the weapons of our warfare are not carnal, but mighty through God to the pulling down of strong holds;) Casting down imaginations, and every high thing that exalteth itself against the knowledge of God, and bringing into captivity every thought to the obedience of Christ.

This can be done through prayers. The enemies' communication system should be destroyed so that their coordination can be disturbed.

Prayer Points

1. Let the communication systems of witchcraft powers be destroyed by fire, in the name of Jesus.
2. Every transportation system of witchcraft powers, be disrupted, in the name of Jesus.
3. Let the weapons of witchcraft powers turn against them, in the name of Jesus.
4. I withdraw my blessings from every bank or strongroom of the enemy, in the name of Jesus.
5. Altar of witchcraft, break, in the name of Jesus.
6. Every witchcraft padlock fashioned against me, break by fire, in the name of Jesus.
7. Every trap of witchcraft, catch your owners, in Jesus' name.
8. Every witchcraft utterance and projection made against me, be

overthrown, in the name of Jesus.

9. I reverse every witchcraft burial fashioned against me, in the name of Jesus.
10. I deliver my soul from every witchcraft bewitchment, in the name of Jesus.
11. I reverse the effect of every witchcraft summoning of my spirit, in the name of Jesus.
12. Every witchcraft identification mark, be wiped off by the blood of Jesus.
13. I frustrate every witchcraft exchange of my virtues, in the name of Jesus.
14. Let the blood of Jesus block the flying route of witchcraft powers targeted against me.
15. Let every witchcraft curse break, in Jesus' name.
16. Every covenant of witchcraft, melt by the blood of Jesus.
17. I withdraw every organ of my body from any witchcraft altar, in the name of Jesus.
18. Anything planted in my life by witchcraft, come out now and die, in the name of Jesus.
19. Let the blood of Jesus cancel every witchcraft initiation fashioned against my destiny, in the name of Jesus.

OFFENSIVE WARFARE

There are two types of warfare: defensive and offensive. In defensive warfare, you defend your territory, while in offensive warfare you launch an attack against the enemy

RULE NUMBER 43 - KEEP YOUR WARFARE STRATEGIES AND PLANS SECRET

Proverb 6:2 says:

Thou art snared with the words of thy mouth, thou art taken with the words of thy mouth.

Proverb 12:12-14 says:

The wicked desireth the net of evil men: but the root of the righteous yieldeth fruit. The wicked is snared by the transgression of his lips: but the just shall come out of trouble. A man shall be satisfied with good by the fruit of his mouth: and the recompence of a man's hands shall be rendered unto him.

There are things not to say or declare publicly as they would empower your opponent. Some people use their mouth to destroy their blessings or speak negative words in the presence of their enemy and he would start immediately to work against them.

Prayer Points

1. Let the fear of me fill the mind of the enemies and let them panic, in the name Jesus.
2. My year shall not be in struggle but in prosperity, in Jesus' name.
3. Let the oppressors drown in their own Red Sea, in Jesus' name.
4. I receive power to leap over every wall that the enemy has built, in the name of Jesus.
5. Let the enemy fall into his own trap, in the name of Jesus
6. Lord, make my miracle invisible to my enemies.
7. Lord, re-organise my system to confuse evil observers.
8. I resist all spiritual sabotage and cunning attacks, in the name Jesus.
9. Let the fire of God protect my miracle, in the name Jesus.
10. Let the root of every night terror dry up, in the name Jesus.
11. Let all the weapons of the enemies work against them, in the name Jesus.
12. The mockery of my enemies shall result in my advancement, in the name Jesus.
13. Lord, turn my morning to dancing and my tears to joy.
14. Let the sword and pit of the enemy turn against him, in the name Jesus.

RULE NUMBER 44 - ALWAYS ATTACK BY FIRE

2 Kings 18:22-24 says:

But if ye say unto me, We trust in the LORD our God: is not that he, whose high places and whose altars Hezekiah hath taken away, and hath said to Judah and Jerusalem, Ye shall worship before this altar in Jerusalem? Now therefore, I pray thee, give pledges to my lord the king of Assyria, and

I will deliver thee two thousand horses, if thou be able on thy part to set riders upon them. How then wilt thou turn away the face of one captain of the least of my master's servants, and put thy trust on Egypt for charlots and for horsemen?

You must attack by fire because God himself is a God that answers by fire.

Prayer Points

1. Let the fire of God destroy all evil registers containing information about my life, in the name of Jesus.
2. Holy Ghost fire, melt away every satanic deposit in my life, in the name of Jesus.
3. Let my oppressors come against one another, in the name of Jesus.
4. Every placental-mediated problem, receive solution now, in the name of Jesus.
5. I break every evil control over my life, in the name of Jesus.
6. I close every tap of sorrow in my life, in the name of Jesus.
7. Let the powers stealing the honey of my life be paralysed, in the name of Jesus.
8. I nullify all spiritual poisons, in the name of Jesus.
9. Let evil satanic worm die, in the name of Jesus.
10. Holy Ghost fire, destroy all satanic poisons in my body, in the name of Jesus.
11. I declare holy rebellion against the forces of oppression working against my life, in the name of Jesus.
12. I possess divine hatred against local wickedness, in Jesus' name.
13. I refuse to follow any satanic road map for my life, in Jesus' name.
14. I defy every satanic army and I command it to bow, in the name of Jesus.
15. I destroy the pride of the enemy over my life, in the name of Jesus.
16. Let my God answer all my evil challengers by fire, in Jesus' name.

17. I break up every satanic concrete caging my potentials, in the name of Jesus.

RULE NUMBER 45 - EXPLOIT EVERY OPPORTUNITY THAT ARISES

2 Cor. 12:4-11 says:

How that he was caught up into paradise, and heard unspeakable words, which it is not lawful for a man to utter. Of such an one will I glory: yet of myself I will not glory, but in mine infirmities. For though I would desire to glory, I shall not be a fool; for I will say the truth: but now I forbear, lest any man should think of me above that which he seeth me to be, or that he heareth of me. And lest I should be exalted above measure through the abundance of the revelations, there was given to me a thorn in the flesh, the messenger of Satan to buffet me, lest I should be exalted above measure. For this thing I besought the Lord thrice, that it might depart from me. And he said unto me, My grace is sufficient for thee: for my strength is made perfect in weakness. Most gladly

You must make good use of every opportunity you have. If you have the gift of prophecy or speaking in tongues use it to disarm your enemies.

Prayer Points

1. Where is the God of Elijah? Arise and pursue my pursuers.
2. Every power closing the gate of breakthroughs against me, what are you waiting for? Die, in the name of Jesus
3. Holy Ghost fire, fire of deliverance, deliver me by fire, in the name of Jesus.
4. Every garment of bondage on my spiritual body, burn to ashes, in the name of Jesus.
5. Every branch of witchcraft in my family tree, die, in the name of Jesus.
6. Every evil covenant which my father's house made with satan, die, in the name of Jesus.
7. Every power of household wickedness working against me, die, in the

name of Jesus.

8. Star of my destiny, arise and shine, in the name of Jesus.
9. Every yoke of hardship working against me, be broken, in the name of Jesus.
10. Every serpent and scorpion swallowing my benefits, vomit them and die, in the name of Jesus.
11. All my blessings imprisoned by the grave, come forth, in the name of Jesus.
12. I release my blessings from the hands of any dead relatives, in the name of Jesus.
13. I withdraw my blessings from the hands of all dead enemies, in the name of Jesus.
14. I disgrace every witchcraft burial, in the name of Jesus.
15. Just as the grave could not detain Jesus, no power can detain my miracles, in the name of Jesus.
16. That which hinders me from greatness, give way now, in the name of Jesus.
17. Whatsoever has been done against me using the ground, be neutralised, in the name of Jesus.
18. Every unfriendly friend, be exposed, in the name of Jesus.
19. Anything representing my image in the spirit world, I withdraw you, in the name of Jesus.
20. All the camps of my enemies, receive confusion, in the name of Jesus.
21. Lord, empower my life with Your authority over every demonic force that set themselves against my life.

RULE NUMBER 46 - ESTABLISH A POWERFUL SECRET INTELLIGENCE SYSTEM

2 Kings 6:8-12 says:

Then the king of Syria warred against Israel, and took counsel with his

servants, saying, In such and such a place shall be my camp. And the man of God sent unto the king of Israel, saying, Beware that thou pass not such a place; for thither the Syrians are come down. And the king of Israel sent to the place which the man of God told him and warned him of, and saved himself there, not once nor twice. Therefore the heart of the king of Syria was sore troubled for this thing; and he called his servants, and said unto them, Will ye not shew me which of us is for the king of Israel? And one of his servants said, None, my lord, O king: but Elisha, the prophet that is in Israel, telleth the king of Israel the words that thou speakest in thy bedchamber.

All governments of the world spend so much money to train spies and intelligence agents to gather information for them. For the believer, the spy is the Holy Spirit who is the greatest of all spies. It was this spy that was at work and the king of Syria wondered who revealed information about his plans to the king of Israel.

Prayer Points

1. I command all the dark works done against my life in secret to be exposed and be nullified, in the name of Jesus.
2. I loose myself from any evil spirit, in the name of Jesus.
3. Lord, if my life is on the wrong course, correct me, in the name of Jesus.
4. Let every anti-progress altar fashioned against me be destroyed with the thunder fire of God, in the name of Jesus.
5. I command my destiny to change to the best, in Jesus' name.
6. Let my hand become a sword of fire to cut down demonic trees, in the name of Jesus.
7. All boasting powers delegated against me, be silenced permanently, in the name of Jesus.
8. I withdraw all my benefits from the hands of the oppressors, in the name of Jesus.
9. Let all unprofitable marks in my life be erased, in Jesus' name.

10. Let every power chasing away my blessings be paralysed, in the name of Jesus.
11. Every good thing belonging to me that has been eaten up by the enemy, be vomited now, in the name of Jesus.
12. Let the anointing for spiritual breakthrough fall upon me, in the name of Jesus.
13. Lord, make me a prayer addict, in the name of Jesus.
14. Lord, ignite my prayer life with Your fire, in the name of Jesus.
15. Lord, empower my prayer altar, in the name of Jesus.
16. I reject every spiritual contamination, in the name of Jesus.
17. Lord, give me power to overcome all obstacles to my breakthroughs, in the name of Jesus.
18. Lord, give me divine prescription for my problems, in the name of Jesus.
19. I break all curses of leaking blessings, in the name of Jesus.
20. Let all spiritual holes in my life be closed with the blood of Jesus, in the name of Jesus.

PRINCIPLES OF SUCCESSFUL WARFARE

We have discussed certain principles that you must come to grips with when you are aiming to obtain victory. A further examination of these principles is the subject of this crucial chapter.

RULE NUMBER 47 - GOOD INFORMATION IS ESSENTIAL FOR SUCCESS

Proverb 20:18 says:

Every purpose is established by counsel: and with good advice make war.

You need good information. You must buy and read good books. You should also listen to life-changing messages and gather information from every possible angle to improve yourself.

RULE NUMBER 48 - LEARN HOW TO CARRY-OUT CIRCULAR ATTACKS

Eph 6:10-13 says:

Finally, my brethren, be strong in the Lord, and in the power of his might. Put on the whole armour of God, that ye may be able to stand against the

wiles of the devil. For we wrestle not against flesh and blood, but against principalities, against powers, against the rulers of the darkness of this world, against spiritual wickedness in high places. Wherefore take unto you the whole armour of God, that ye may be able to withstand in the evil day, and having done all, to stand.

This means analysing and attacking everything about the enemy. Attack everything that empowers the enemy.

Prayer Points

1. Lord, grant me the power to be fulfilled, successful and prosperous, in the name of Jesus.
2. Lord, break me up in every department of my life and remould me, in the name of Jesus.
3. Lord, make me to break through into dumfounding miracles in all areas of my life, in the name of Jesus.
4. Lord, make me to break out of every obstacle on my way to progress, in the name of Jesus.
5. Lord, establish me in truth, godliness and faithfulness.
6. Lord, add flavour to my work, in the name of Jesus.
7. Lord, add increase to my work, in the name of Jesus.
8. Lord, add profitability to my work, in the name Jesus.
9. Lord, promote and preserve my life, in the name of Jesus
10. I reject the plans and agenda of the enemies against my life, in the name of Jesus.
11. I reject the assignments and weapons of the enemy against my life, in the name of Jesus.
12. Let every weapon and evil design against me fail totally, in the name of Jesus.
13. I reject premature death, in the name of Jesus.
14. I reject nightmares and sudden destruction, in the name of Jesus.

15. I reject dryness in my walk with God, in the name of Jesus.

16. I reject financial debt, in the name of Jesus.

17. I reject lack and famine in my life, in the name of Jesus.

18. I reject physical and spiritual accidents in my going in and coming out, in the name of Jesus.

RULE NUMBER 49 - FIGHT STEP BY STEP AND PRECEPT UPON PRECEPT

Isaiah 28:10-13 says:

For precept must be upon precept, precept upon precept; line upon line, line upon line; here a little, and there a little: For with stammering lips and another tongue will he speak to this people. To whom he said, This is the rest wherewith ye may cause the weary to rest; and this is the refreshing: yet they would not hear. But the word of the LORD was unto them precept upon precept, precept upon precept; line upon line, line upon line; here a little, and there a little; that they might go, and fall backward, and be broken, and snared, and taken.

Let your fight be in this order. Write down your battles and pray over them one by one. General things do not work. Perhaps, you come from a home where there is trouble and there are several problems facing you now, you must deal with them one after the other.

Prayer Points

1. Let each step my enemies take lead them to greater destruction, in the name of Jesus.
2. But as for me, let me dwell in the hollow of God's hand, in the name of Jesus.
3. Let the goodness and mercies of God overwhelm me now, in the name of Jesus.
4. Any witchcraft practised under any water against my life, receive immediate judgment of fire, in the name of Jesus.

5. Every witchcraft power that has introduced spirit husband/wife or child into my dreams, be roasted by firer, in the name of Jesus.
6. Every agent of witchcraft power posing as my husband, wife or child in my dreams, be roasted by fire, in the name of Jesus.
7. Every agent of witchcraft power physically attached to my marriage to frustrate it, fall down and perish now, in the name of Jesus.
8. Every agent of witchcraft power assigned to attack my finances through dream, fall down and perish, in the name of Jesus.
9. Let the thunderbolts of God locate and destroy every witchcraft power covens where deliberations and decisions are fashioned against me, in the name of Jesus.
10. Any water spirit from my village, or from the place of my birth, practising witchcraft against me and my family, be amputated by the word of God, in the name of Jesus.

RULE NUMBER 50 - DO NOT COMPLAIN OR COMPARE AND CONTRAST BUT FOCUS ON THE BATTLE

2 Cor 10:12 says:

For we dare not make ourselves of the number, or compare ourselves with some that commend themselves: but they measuring themselves by themselves, and comparing themselves among themselves, are not wise.

You must not compare your life with another's life. Do not complain about your destiny. Do not compare and contrast. Be focused on the battle.

Prayer Points

1. I command my battle to change to blessings, in Jesus' name.
2. Let every mountain of satanic confrontation be disgraced, in the name of Jesus.
3. Let every mountain of impossibility be dashed to pieces, in the name of Jesus.

4. Let new wells spring up in my desert, in the name of Jesus.
5. Lord, bear me up on eagle's wings before my enemies.
6. Lord, anoint my eyes to see my divine opportunities.
7. I refuse to allow my present to influence my future negatively.
8. Let every satanic battle confronting me fall apart, in Jesus' name.
9. I throw down the strongman of financial embarrassment, in Jesus' name.
10. I declare myself free from the plagues of spiritual Egypt, in the name of Jesus.
11. I command all crooked and difficult areas of my life to begin to yield testimonies, in the name of Jesus.
12. Let the spirit of excellence manifest in every areas of my life, in the name of Jesus.
13. Let the fear of me fill the minds of my enemies and let them panic, in the name of Jesus.
14. My year shall not be in struggle but in prosperity, in Jesus' name.
15. Let the oppressors drown in their own Red Sea, in Jesus' name.
16. I receive power to leap over every wall that the enemy has built, in the name of Jesus.
17. Let the enemy fall into his own trap, in the name of Jesus
18. Lord, make my miracle invisible to my enemies.
19. Lord, reorganise my system to confuse evil observers.
20. I resist all spiritual sabotage and cunning attacks, in the name of Jesus.
21. Let the fire of God protect my miracle, in the name of Jesus.
22. Let the root of every night terror dry up, in the name of Jesus.

RULE NUMBER 51 - ENSURE ADEQUATE WORD LEVEL

Colossians 3:16 says:

Let the word of Christ dwell in you richly in all wisdom; teaching and admonishing one another in psalms and hymns and spiritual songs, singing

with grace in your hearts to the Lord.

You must mediate on the Scripture and memorise warfare Scriptures copiously. Begin to say those words and not too long a time they will become part and parcel of you and if anyone wages war against you, you can silence him immediately.

Prayer Points

1. I bind every word spoken against my breakthroughs, in the name of Jesus.
2. Every business house energised by satan, fold up, in the name of Jesus.
3. I destroy every clock and time-table of poverty, in Jesus' name.
4. Every water spirit, touch not my prosperity, in the name of Jesus.
5. Let men and women rush wealth to my doors, in Jesus' name.
6. I reject temporary blessings, in the name of Jesus.
7. Every arrow of poverty energised by polygamy, fall down and die, in the name of Jesus.
8. Every arrow of poverty energised by household wickedness, fall down and die, in the name of Jesus.
9. Let power change hands in my finances, in the name of Jesus.
10. Every serpent and scorpion of poverty, die, in the name of Jesus.
11. I refuse to eat the bread of sorrow and I reject the water of affliction, in the name of Jesus.
12. Let divine explosion fall upon my breakthroughs, in Jesus' name.
13. The enemy will not drag my finances on the ground, in the name of Jesus.
14. Lord, advertise your wealth and power in my life.
15. Let promotion meet promotion in my life, in the name of Jesus.
16. I pursue and overtake my enemy and recover my wealth from him, in the name of Jesus.
17. Holy Spirit, direct my hands into prosperity, in the name of Jesus.

COMPLETE VICTORY IN SPIRITUAL WARFARE

No matter how numerous or strong your battles are, you can experience complete victory. Your victory can be so complete that you will become a threat to the kingdom of darkness.

RULE NUMBER 52 - PUT ON THE WHOLE ARMOUR OF GOD.

Ephesians 6:12-8 says:

For we wrestle not against flesh and blood, but against principalities, against powers, against the rulers of the darkness of this world, against spiritual wickedness in high places. Wherefore take unto you the whole armour of God, that ye may be able to withstand in the evil day, and having done all, to stand. Stand therefore, having your loins girt about with truth, and having on the breastplate of righteousness; And your feet shod with the preparation of the gospel of peace; Above all, taking the shield of faith, wherewith ye shall be able to quench all the fiery darts of the wicked. And take the helmet of salvation, and the sword of the Spirit, which is the word of God: Praying always with all prayer and supplication in the Spirit, and watching thereunto with all perseverance and supplication for all saints.

Truth, righteousness, salvation and prayer are the armour of God.

Prayer Points

1. I command the armour of the strongman to be roasted completely, in the name of Jesus.
2. I command all curses issued against me to be smashed and broken, in the name of Jesus.
3. I separate my life from all evil idols present in my place of birth, in the name of Jesus.
4. I separate my life from evil streams present in my place of birth, in the name of Jesus.
5. I separate my life from all evil shrines present in my place of birth, in the name of Jesus.
6. Let all agents banking my blessing release them now, in the name of Jesus.
7. I destroy every evil peace, evil agreement, evil unity, evil love, evil happiness, evil understanding, evil communication and evil gathering fashioned against my life, in Jesus' name.
8. Let every power of the oppressor rise up against each other, in the name of Jesus.
9. I disband all evil host gathered against my progress, in the name of Jesus.
10. Let the sorrow of the enemy upon the progress of my life remain permanent, in the name of Jesus.
11. Let all drinkers of blood and eaters of flesh hunting for my life stumble and fall, in the name of Jesus.
12. I paralyse all problem expanders, in the name of Jesus.
13. I paralyse all forces behind delayed miracle, in Jesus' name.
14. Thank God for answer to your prayer.

RULE NUMBER 53 - ALWAYS FOLLOW THE PRINCIPLE OF OPERATION P-U-S-H

Rom 12:12 says:

Rejoicing in hope; patient in tribulation; continuing instant in prayer.

Luke 6:12 says:

And it came to pass in those days, that he went out into a mountain to pray, and continued all night in prayer to God.

Col 4:2 says:

Continue in prayer, and watch in the same with thanksgiving.

This is praying until something happens. You must not relent in your prayer life.

Prayer Points

1. I push out every plantation of darkness in my womb, in Jesus' name'
2. Every deposit of darkness, loose your hold, in Jesus' name
3. Every evil hand laid upon my womb, roast, in Jesus' name.
4. Anything planted in my womb to drink my blood, come out now, in the name of Jesus.
5. I shall not incubate any property of darkness in my womb, in the name of Jesus.
6. Womb polluters, loose your hold, in the name of Jesus.
7. Anything planted in my life that is contrary to the will of God, be uprooted now, in the name of Jesus.
8. I bind and cast out any dark spirit moving about in my womb, in the name of Jesus.
9. Fire of God, destroy every plantation of infirmity in my womb, in the name of Jesus.
10. Every blood-drinking demon assigned against my womb, I bind and cast you out, in the name of Jesus.

11. Every conspiracy against my vessel of reproduction, be scattered, in the name of Jesus.
12. God, arise and let every enemy of my marital bliss scatter, in the name of Jesus.
13. My womb, depart from the hold of every altar of darkness, in the name of Jesus.
14. Every burden in my womb, be dissolved, in the name of Jesus.
15. Every yoke in my womb, break, in the name of Jesus.

RULE NUMBER 54 - ALWAYS GET A WORD FROM THE LORD

Jer 37:17 says:

Then Zedekiah the king sent, and took him out: and the king asked him secretly in his house, and said, Is there any word from the LORD? And Jeremiah said, There is: for, said he, thou shalt be delivered into the hand of the king of Babylon.

Do not start fighting your battles until you have heard a word from the Lord.

Prayer Points

1. Let every secret about battle against my spiritual life be revealed, in the name of Jesus.
2. I reject and release myself from the grip of the spirit of infirmity, in the name of Jesus.
3. I drink the blood of Jesus into the whole of my system.
4. Lord, build around me the hedge of fire.
5. Let the spirit of life replace the spirit of death in my life, in the name of Jesus.
6. Woe unto the demonic vessel that the enemy may use to cause me spiritual injury, in the name of Jesus.
7. Father Lord, let your glory cover every aspect of my life, in the name of Jesus.
8. Father Lord, let your angels encamp around me, in Jesus' name.

9. I renounce and break every death covenant that have made or which anyone has made on my behalf, in Jesus' name.
10. I remove the control of my life from the hands of any dead person, in the name of Jesus.
11. I stand against every covenant of sudden death, in Jesus' name.
12. Every blessing of mine that has been buried in the ground or under the water, be revealed by fire, in Jesus' name.
13. I cancel my name from every death register, in Jesus' name.
14. I stand against every form of tragedy, in Jesus' name.
15. Every grave cloth over my life, be removed by fire, in Jesus' name.
16. All my potentials that have been destroyed, revive by fire, in Jesus' name.
17. I stand against all the powers that push a person to hell fire, in the name of Jesus.

RULE NUMBER 55 - A DISARMED SOLDIER REPRESENTS A WEAK AND USUALLY DEFEATED NATION

Phil 3:14-19 says:

I press toward the mark for the prize of the high calling of God in Christ Jesus. Let us therefore, as many as be perfect, be thus minded: and if in any thing ye be otherwise minded, God shall reveal even this unto you. Nevertheless, whereto we have already attained, let us walk by the same rule, let us mind the same thing. Brethren, be followers together of me, and mark them which walk so as ye have us for an ensample. (For many walk, of whom I have told you often, and now tell you even weeping, that they are the enemies of the cross of Christ: Whose end is destruction, whose God is their belly, and whose glory is in their shame, who mind earthly things.)

Once a soldier is disarmed, a weak and a defeated nation will follow. Once the enemy takes away your weapon, the battle is over and to the enemy's advantage. It is my prayer for you that the enemy shall not locate your weapon

Prayer Points

1. Every battle waged against me by the kingdom of darkness, receive defeat, in the mighty name of Jesus.
2. Distributors of spiritual poison, swallow your poison, in the name of Jesus.
3. All forces of Egypt in my life, rise up against yourselves, in the name of Jesus.
4. Father Lord, let the joy of the enemy over my life be turned to sorrow.
5. You demonic armies stationed against my life, receive the judgment of leprosy, in the name of Jesus
6. I command the evil power source in my place of birth to be destroyed completely, in the name of Jesus.
7. Every access to my life by the enemy, I block you, in the name of Jesus
8. Every problem that came into my life by personal invitation, depart, in the name of Jesus.

RULE NUMBER 56 -YOU MUST DIRECT ANGELS INTO YOUR BATTLE BY ISSUING DECREES

Hebrew 1:13-14 says:

But to which of the angels said he at any time, Sit on my right hand, until I make thine enemies thy footstool? Are they not all ministering spirits, sent forth to minister for them who shall be heirs of salvation?

The Bible says that angels are our ministers. We must make use of them in battle.

Prayer Points

1. Let the warring angels and the Spirit of God arise and scatter every evil gathering sponsored against me, in the name of Jesus.
2. I disobey any satanic order programmed by inheritance into my life, in

the name of Jesus

3. I bind and cast out every power causing internal warfare, in the name of Jesus.
4. Every demonic doorkeeper locking out good things for me, be paralysed by fire, in the name of Jesus.
5. I command every evil power fighting against me to fight against themselves and destroy one another, in Jesus' name.
6. Every breakthrough hindering, delaying, preventing and breaking demon, receive confusion, in the name of Jesus.
7. Let divine power and control attack the spirits of violence and torture, in the name of Jesus.
8. Let the spirits of witchcraft and familiar spirits fashioned against me die, in the name of Jesus.
9. Let there be a civil war in the kingdom of darkness, in the name of Jesus.
10. Lord, loose judgement and destruction upon all stubborn and reluctant spirits that fail to obey my commands promptly, in the name of Jesus.

RULE NUMBER 57 - BE SURE OF YOUR SALVATION

I Thes 5:8 says:

But let us, who are of the day, be sober, putting on the breastplate of faith and love; and for an helmet, the hope of salvation.

Eph 6:17 says:

And take the helmet of salvation, and the sword of the Spirit, which is the word of God:

If you are not saved, you will be a casualty on the field of battle. You must be very sure of your salvation.

Prayer Points

1. I grab every stubborn problem and smash them against the Rock of salvation, in the name of Jesus.
2. I nullify every sacrifice to demons used against me, in Jesus' name.
3. Every power cursing my destiny, be silenced, in Jesus' name.
4. I break the power of any incense burnt against me, in Jesus' name.
5. Every python spirit, go into the hot desert and be burned, in the name of Jesus.
6. Let the blood of Jesus poison the roots of all my problems, in the name of Jesus.
7. I got back Adam and Eve on both sides of my bloodline, and I cut down every evil root, in the name of Jesus.
8. I reverse every improper operation of my body organs, in Jesus' name.
9. Every evil contract working against my life, be re-written by the blood of Jesus.
10. I reverse every satanic calendar for my life, in the name of Jesus.
11. Anything my ancestors have done to pollute my life, be dismantled now, in the name of Jesus.
12. I refuse to be at the right place at the wrong time, in Jesus' name.
13. I bind every negative energy in the air, water and ground working against me, in the name of Jesus.
14. Anything from the kingdom of darkness that has made it its business to hinder me, I single you out right now and bind you, in the name of Jesus.
    a. Be bound with chains that cannot be broken, in the name of Jesus.
    b. I strip off all your spiritual armour, in the name of Jesus.
    c. Lose the support of other evil powers, in the name of Jesus.

d.Do not involve yourself with me again, in Jesus' name.

15. Lord Jesus, I thank You for the victory you have given me.

16. I renounced every signing of my name over to satan, in Jesus' name.

RULE NUMBER 58 - BE FILLED WITH THE HOLY SPIRIT

Eph 5:18 says:

And be not drunk with wine, wherein is excess; but be filled with the Spirit.

Do not just rely on the baptism of the Holy Ghost. You must get various baptisms.

Prayer Points

1. Lord, let the fire of the Holy Spirit warm every satanic freeze in my life.
2. Lord, give me a life that kills death.
3. Lord, kindle in me the fire of charity.
4. Lord, glue me together where I am opposed to myself.
5. Lord, enrich me with your gifts.
6. Lord, quicken me and increase my desire for the things of heaven.
2. By your rulership, O Lord, let the lust of the flesh in my life die.
3. Lord Jesus, increase daily in my life.
4. Lord Jesus, maintain your gifts in my life.
5. Lord, refine and purge my heart, in the name of Jesus.
6. Holy Spirit, inflame and fire my heart, in the name of Jesus.
7. Lord Jesus, lay your hands upon me and quench every rebellion in me.
8. Holy Ghost fire, begin to burn away every self-centeredness in me, in the name of Jesus.
9. Father Lord, breathe your life-giving breath into my soul, in the name of Jesus.

10. Lord, make me ready to go wherever you send me.

11. Lord Jesus, never let me shut you out.

12. Lord Jesus, never let me try to limit you to my capacity.

13. Lord Jesus, work freely in me and through me.

14. Lord, purify the channels of my life.

15. Let your heat, O Lord, consume my will, in the name of Jesus.

RULE NUMBER 59 - ENSURE THAT YOU ARE NOT IN POSSESSION OF ANY MATERIAL FROM THE ENEMY

Joshua 7:20-26 says:

And Achan answered Joshua, and said, Indeed I have sinned against the LORD God of Israel, and thus and thus have I done: When I saw among the spoils a goodly Babylonish garment, and two hundred shekels of silver, and a wedge of gold of fifty shekels weight, then I coveted them, and took them; and, behold, they are hid in the earth in the midst of my tent, and the silver under it. So Joshua sent messengers, and they ran unto the tent; and, behold, it was hid in his tent, and the silver under it. And they took them out of the midst of the tent, and brought them unto Joshua, and unto all the children of Israel, and laid them out before the LORD. And Joshua, and all Israel with him, took Achan the son of Zerah, and the silver, and the garment, and the wedge of gold, and his sons, and his daughters, and his oxen, and his asses, and his sheep, and his tent, and all that he had: and they brought them unto the valley of Achor. And Joshua said, Why hast thou troubled us? the LORD shall trouble thee this day. And all Israel stoned him with stones, and burned them with fire, after they had stoned them with stones. And they raised over him a great heap of stones unto this day. So the LORD turned from the fierceness of his anger. Wherefore the name of that place was called, The valley of Achor, unto this day.

Anything in your hand that belongs to the enemy will definitely invite the enemy to you and weaken your position.

Prayer Points

1. I refuse to pick the wrong materials from the bank of life, in the name of Jesus.
2. I refuse to lose any ground in my life to the enemy, in Jesus' name.
3. Let every inherited wicked plantation in my life be uprooted, in the name of Jesus.
4. My prosperity will not become history while I am yet living, in the name of Jesus.
5. I paralyse every progress arrester, in the name of Jesus.
6. Lord, satisfy me till my satisfaction overflows.
7. Let my breakthroughs baffle my enemies, in the name of Jesus.
8. I defy the camp of the enemy with the blood of Jesus.
9. Let every instrument of bewitching be rendered impotent now, in the name of Jesus.
10. You stubborn problems, I trample upon your serpents and scorpions, in the name of Jesus.
11. Let the military angels of the Almighty pursue and attack my attackers, in the name of Jesus.
12. Let confusion be created in the camp of my oppressors, in the name of Jesus.
13. Let every battle in the heavenlies be won in favour of the angels conveying my blessings, in the name of Jesus.
14. Let every satanic law programmed into my life be terminated, in the name of Jesus.
15. Let every evil ancestral law programmed into my genes be terminated, in the name of Jesus.
16. Let my prayers release angelic intervention to my favour, in the name of Jesus.
17. I receive the anointing to disgrace satanic arrows, in Jesus' name
18. I cut off every supply of food to my problems, in the name of Jesus

19. **Let thunder from the Lord destroy every evil altar constructed against me, in the name of Jesus.**
20. **Lord, release me from known and unknown curses.**

SECRETS OF RESOUNDING VICTORY

God has created for every believer a solid platform for victory. You can stand on this platform and fight your way to victory. The rules contained in this chapter are specially vomited by the Holy Ghost

RULE NUMBER 60 - YOU HAVE THE POWER TO CAUSE THE ENEMIES TO DESTROY THEMSELVES.

Psalm 27:1-2 says:

The LORD is my light and my salvation; whom shall I fear? the LORD is the strength of my life; of whom shall I be afraid? When the wicked, even mine enemies and my foes, came upon me to eat up my flesh, they stumbled and fell.

Isaiah 49:26 says:

And I will feed them that oppress thee with their own flesh; and they shall be drunken with their own blood, as with sweet wine: and all flesh shall know that I the LORD am thy Saviour and thy Redeemer, the mighty One of Jacob.

By sponsoring the civil war among the enemies, you can cause them to destroy themselves. In the Scriptures it happened several times when the enemies fought and destroyed themselves.

Prayer Points

1. Lord, heal any hormonal imbalance or other harmful secretions in my body.
2. Lord, heal me in whatever needs to be healed.
3. Lord, replace in me whatever needs to be replaced.
4. Lord, transform me in whatever needs to be transformed.
5. Lord, let your healing power take firm root within me.
6. Let the strongmen from both sides of my family begin to destroy themselves now, in the name of Jesus.
7. The strongman from my father's side and the strongman from my mother's side, destroy yourselves, in the name of Jesus.
8. I refuse to wear the garment of sorrow, in the name of Jesus.
9. All stubborn pursuers in my life, I command you to die, in the name of Jesus.
10. All satanic arrows in my life at present, lose your power, in the name of Jesus.
11. Let every organised evil arrow against my life be paralysed, in the name of Jesus.
12. I fire back all satanic arrows of depression at the edge of my breakthroughs, in the name of Jesus.
13. I fire back all satanic arrows of spiritual and physical sicknesses, in the mime of Jesus.
14. I fire back all satanic arrows of weakness in prayer and Bible reading, in the name of Jesus.
15. I fire back all satanic arrows of business failure, in Jesus' name.
16. I fire back all evil arrows from the household enemy, in the name of Jesus.

17. I fire back all evil arrows from my unfriendly friends, in Jesus' name.
18. Power of God, bring to life all my good benefits that satanic arrows have paralysed, in the name of Jesus
19. I cover my life and all my belongings from satanic arrows by the blood of Jesus.
20. Thank the Lord that the gate of hell shall not prevail against your life.
21. I order confusion and scattering of tongues against all wicked associations militating against the peace of my life, in Jesus' name.
22. Let the wisdom of all evil counsellors in my life be rendered to nothing, in the name of Jesus.

RULE NUMBER 61 - BE CONFIDENT THAT YOU HAVE A GREAT CAPTAIN WHO HAS NEVER LOST A BATTLE

This implies that if you plug yourself to this captain, your victory is assured. Keep contact with God always to ensure victory in your battles.

Prayer Points

1. My destiny is attached to God, therefore, I decree that I can never fail, in the name of Jesus.
2. I refuse to be programmed against my divine destiny, in the name of Jesus.
3. I destroy every record of my destiny in the marine world, in the name of Jesus.
4. Every altar mounted against my destiny in the heavenlies, be dismantled, in the name of Jesus.
5. I reject every satanic alternative for my destiny, in Jesus' name.
6. Evil cauldrons, you will not cook up my destiny, in Jesus' name.
7. I destroy every witchcraft cauldron and concoction against my destiny, in the name of Jesus.
8. Every power of the cauldron raised up to manipulate my destiny, release

me, in the name of Jesus.

9. Destiny swallowers vomit my destiny, in the name of Jesus.
10. I recover my stolen vehicle of destiny, in the name of Jesus.
11. Every conference of darkness against my destiny, scatter, in the name of Jesus.
12. Lord, anoint my destiny afresh.
13. Failure shall not slaughter my destiny, in the name of Jesus.
14. Every power waging war against my destiny, fall down and die, in the name of Jesus.
15. Destiny thieves, release me now, in the name of Jesus.
16. I overthrow every satanic re–arrangement programmed against my destiny, in the name of Jesus.
17. I have come to Zion, my destiny must change, in Jesus' name.
18. Every power derailing my destiny, fall down and die, in the name of Jesus.
19. I refuse to miss my destiny in life, in the name of Jesus.
20. I refuse to accept satanic substitute for my destiny, in the name of Jesus.
21. Anything programmed against my destiny in the heavenlies, be shaken down, in the name of Jesus.

RULE NUMBER 62 - YOUR LEVEL OF COMMITMENT TO THE THINGS OF GOD DETERMINES YOUR SUCCESS

Deut 32:10 says:

He found him in a desert land, and in the waste howling wilderness; he led him about, he instructed him, he kept him as the apple of his eye.

Psalm 17:8-13 says:

Keep me as the apple of the eye, hide me under the shadow of thy wings, From the wicked that oppress me, from my deadly enemies, who compass me about. They are inclosed in their own fat: with their mouth they speak proudly. They have now compassed us in our steps: they have set their eyes

bowing down to the earth; Like as a lion that is greedy of his prey, and as it were a young lion lurking in secret places. Arise, O LORD, disappoint him, cast him down: deliver my soul from the wicked, which is thy sword.

God will not allow the apple of His eyes to be disgraced.

Prayer Points

1. Oh Lord, give unto me the key to good success, so that anywhere I go the doors of good success will be opened unto me.
2. Let every wicked house constructed against me and my career be demolished, in the name of Jesus.
3. Oh Lord, establish me as a holy person unto You, in Jesus' name.
4. Oh Lord, let the anointing to excel in my career fall on me, in the name of Jesus.
5. I shall not serve my enemies; my enemies shall bow down to me, in the name of Jesus.
6. I bind every desert and poverty spirit in my life, in Jesus' name.
7. I reject the anointing of non-achievement in my career, in the name of Jesus.
8. I pull down all the strongholds erected against my progress, in the name of Jesus.
9. I recall all my blessings thrown into water, forest and satanic bank, in the name of Jesus.
10. I cut down all the roots of problems in my life, in the name of Jesus.
11. Let satanic scorpions be rendered stingless in every area of my life, in the name of Jesus.
12. Let demonic serpents be rendered venomless in every area of my life, in the name of Jesus.
13. I declare with my mouth that nothing shall be impossible with me, in the name of Jesus.
14. Let the camp of the enemy be put in disarray, in the name of Jesus.

15. Spiritual parasites in my life, be disgraced, in the name of Jesus.
16. Let all my Herods receive spiritual decay, in the name of Jesus.
17. Oh Lord, let Your favour and that of man encompass me on my career this year, in Jesus' name.

RULE NUMBER 63 - THE FRUITS OF THE SPIRIT IN YOUR LIFE MAKES YOU UNTOUCHABLE

Eph 5:9 says:

For the fruit of the Spirit is in all goodness and righteousness and truth.

Gal 5:22 says:

But the fruit of the Spirit is love, joy, peace, longsuffering, gentleness, goodness, faith,

You need the fruits of the spirit as a solder.

Prayer Points

1. I shall not labour in vain. Another person shall not eat the fruit of my labour, in the name of Jesus.
2. Every ancestral spirit of anger, loose your hold upon my life, in the name of Jesus.
3. Every hold of unforgiving spirit in my life, break by the blood of Jesus.
4. Every hold of the spirit of prayerlessness in my life, die now, in the name of Jesus.
5. Every spirit stealing from me, fall down and die, in the name of Jesus.
6. Every spirit of blindness in my life, die, in the name of Jesus.
7. Every spirit of poverty in my foundation, die, in the name of Jesus.
8. Every problem planned for my future, you shall not see the daylight, in the name of Jesus.
9. Every warfare against my breakthroughs in the heavenlies, scatter, in the name of Jesus.

10. Let every cycle of problems in my life die, in the name of Jesus.
11. By the blood of Jesus, I make my breakthroughs untouchable for any evil powers, in the name of Jesus.
12. You powers working against my treasures, fall down and die, in the name of Jesus.
13. Thank God for answers to your prayers.
14. Thank God for making provision for deliverance from any form of bondage.
15. Confess your sins and those of your ancestors, especially those sins linked to evil powers.
16. I cover myself with the blood of Jesus.
17. I release myself from any inherited bondage, in Jesus' name.
18. Lord, send Your axe of fire to the foundation of my life and destroy every evil plantation.
19. Let the blood of Jesus flush out from my system every inherited satanic deposit, in the name of Jesus.

RULE NUMBER 64 - A FEARFUL HEART IS ALREADY A CASUALTY

Proverb 29:25 says:

The fear of man bringeth a snare: but whoso putteth his trust in the LORD shall be safe.

Banish fear from your heart.

Prayer Points

1. By the blood of Jesus, I rebuke every attacking and fearful dream, in the name of Jesus.
2. Let the evil vision and dream on my life evaporate and condense in the camp of the enemy, in the name of Jesus.
3. Every cause of demotion in the dream in my life, be nullified by the blood of Jesus.

4. Every cause of confused and unprogressive dreams in my life, be nullified by the blood of Jesus.
5. Every cause of being harassed in the dreams by familiar faces, be nullified by the blood of Jesus.
6. I send the arrows and any gun shot in the dream back to the senders, in the name of Jesus.
7. I paralyse all the night caterers and I forbid their food in my dream, in the name of Jesus.
8. All pursuers in my dreams, begin to pursue yourself, in Jesus' name.
9. Let all the contamination in my life through dreams be cleansed by the blood of Jesus
10. I cancel every dream of backwardness, in the name of Jesus
11. Every dream of demotion to junior school, be dismantled.
12. I shall go from glory to glory, in the name of Jesus.
13. By the power in the blood of Jesus, I cancel the maturity dates of any evil dreams in my life.
14. You God of promotion, promote me beyond my widest dreams, in the name of Jesus.
15. Every sickness planted through the dream into my life, get out now and go back to your sender, in the name of Jesus.
16. Let life be squeezed out of my dream attackers, in Jesus' name.
17. By the power in the blood of Jesus, I command all my buried good dreams and visions to be exhumed.

RULE NUMBER 65 - YOU MUST MAKE UP YOUR MIND

2 Tim 2:3-5 says:

Thou therefore endure hardness, as a good soldier of Jesus Christ. No man that warreth entangleth himself with the affairs of this life; that he may please him who hath chosen him to be a soldier. And if a man also strive for masteries, yet is he not crowned, except he strive lawfully.

You have to decide. God does not decide for you. You must make up your mind to fight the battle.

Prayer Points

1. Let God arise in His anger and wage my war for me, in Jesus' name.
2. I neutralise all problems originating from the mistakes of my parents, in the name of Jesus.
3. I neutralise all problems originating from my past mistakes, in the name of Jesus.
4. Lord, bring honey out of the rock for me this month, in the name of Jesus.
5. Lord, open all the good doors of my life that household wickedness has shut, in the name of Jesus.
6. Let all anti-breakthrough designs against my life be shattered to irreparable pieces, in the name of Jesus.
7. I paralyse all satanic antagonism against my destiny right from the womb, in the name of Jesus.
8. I trample upon every enemy of my advancement and I unseat all evil powers sitting on my promotions, in the name of Jesus.
9. Lord, enlarge my coast beyond my wildest dreams, in the name of Jesus.
10. I claim back all my goods residing in wrong hands at present, in the name of Jesus.
11. Lord, uproot from my life the evil things that are against my advancement, in the name of Jesus.
12. Lord, plant into my life good things that will advance my cause, in the name of Jesus.
13. Let every spiritual weakness in my life receive permanent termination, in the name of Jesus.
14. Let every financial failure in my life receive permanent termination, in the name of Jesus
15. Let every sickness fashioned to pull my advancement down receive

permanent termination, in the name of Jesus.

16. Let every architect of problems against my advancement receive permanent termination, in the name of Jesus.

RULE NUMBER 66 - YOUR CONFIDENCE MUST BE IN THE LORD ALONE

Isaiah 51:9 says:

Awake, awake, put on strength, O arm of the LORD; awake, as in the ancient days, in the generations of old. Art thou not it that hath cut Rahab, and wounded the dragon?

Isaiah 53:1 says:

Who hath believed our report? and to whom is the arm of the LORD revealed?

2 Chro 32:8 says:

With him is an arm of flesh; but with us is the LORD our God to help us, and to fight our battles. And the people rested themselves upon the words of Hezekiah king of Judah.

Do not mix self-confidence with confidence in God. Do not put your confidence in someone else except God. You must believe in Him alone.

Prayer Points

1. O Lord, enlarge my coast.
2. Let every embargo on my progress fall down and scatter, in the name of Jesus.
3. I reject satanic restrictions in every area of my life, in the name of Jesus.
4. Let the mighty hands of God be upon me for good, in Jesus' name.
5. Lord, keep me from all evil wisdom and manipulation.
6. I reject any invitation to appointment with sorrow, in Jesus' name.
7. I scatter evil multitudes gathered against me, in the name of Jesus.

8. Let God be God against my oppressors, in the name of Jesus.
9. The Lord will not be a spectator in my affairs, but a participant, in the name of Jesus.
10. Lord, save me from drowning in the sea of life.
11. My head will not be anchored to doubt, in the name of Jesus.
12. I refuse any evil diversion, in the name of Jesus.
13. I will not take my eyes off the Lord Jesus, in the name of Jesus.
14. Lord, anchor your mercy to my head.
15. Lord Jesus, let me receive the touch of signs and wonders now.
16. Let God be God in my Red Sea situation, in the name of Jesus.
17. God, let it be known that You are' God in every department of my life, in the name of Jesus.
18. Lord, do a new thing to my enemies that would permanently dismantle their power.
19. Lord, let uncommon techniques be utilised to disgrace any opposition against my life.
20. Let the earth open up and swallow every stubborn pursuer in my life, in the name of Jesus.
21. Lord God of Abraham, Isaac and Jacob, manifest Yourself in Your power to bless me.
22. Lord, begin to answer every evil stronghold by fire and burn them to ashes.
23. Every power challenging the power of God in my life, be disgraced now, in the name of Jesus.
24. Let every rage of the enemy against my coming breakthroughs be disgraced now, in the name of Jesus. .

ANOINTING FOR VICTORY

You need the warfare anointing as a believer. The concluding rules in this chapter will place a divine seal on your victory

RULE NUMBER 67 - PROCEED UNDER THE ANOINTING

Isaiah 10:27 says:

And it shall come to pass in that day, that his burden shall be taken away from off thy shoulder, and his yoke from off thy neck, and the yoke shall be destroyed because of the anointing.

It is by the anointing that the yoke will be broken. So, you must proceed on every battle under the anointing.

Prayer Points

1. Every anointing of desert spirit upon my life, dry up by the fire of the Holy Ghost, in the name of Jesus.
2. Blood of Jesus, block every doorway of poverty, in the name of Jesus.
3. All the powers assisting poverty in my life, be bound, in the name of Jesus.

4. My life, receive the anointing of fruitfulness, in the name of Jesus.
5. My life, refuse to be anchored to any evil, in the name of Jesus.
6. My head, refuse to bear any evil burden, in the name of Jesus.
7. I refuse to walk into any problem, in the name of Jesus.
8. My hands, refuse to magnetise problem to me, in Jesus' name.
9. Every satanic architect of problems assigned against me, be roasted, in the name of Jesus.
10. I break the backbone of any problem associated with every second of my life, in the name of Jesus.
11. Any power that has been supplying strength to problems in my life, be wasted, in the name of Jesus.
12. I refuse to swim in the ocean of problems, in the name of Jesus.
13. Every remotely controlled problem energised by household wickedness, be devoured by the Lion of Judah, in Jesus' name.
14. I sack and disband any power behind the problems of my life, in the name of Jesus.
15. Lord Jesus, I refuse to be kept busy by the devil.
16. I receive power to convert failures designed for my life to outstanding successes, in the name of Jesus.
17. I receive power to close down every satanic factory designed for me, in the name of Jesus.

RULE NUMBER 68 - SHOW NO MERCY TO UNREPENTANT ENEMIES

Deut 19:13 says:

Thine eye shall not pity him, but thou shalt put away the guilt of innocent blood from Israel, that it may go well with thee.

Deut 19:21 says:

And thine eye shall not pity; but life shall go for life, eye for eye, tooth for tooth, hand for hand, foot for foot.

Deut 25:12 says:

Then thou shalt cut off her hand, thine eye shall not pity her.

If you show mercy to unrepentant enemies, the mercy will be to your disadvantage.

Prayer Points

1. I command my destiny to reject every bewitchment, in the name of Jesus.
2. I deliver my destiny from the grip of destiny killers, in Jesus' name.
3. Every evil done to my destiny by household wickedness, be reversed now, in the name of Jesus.
4. Every vessel of destiny killers fashioned against my destiny, fall down and die, in the name of Jesus.
5. Let the ground open now and swallow all destiny killers working against me, in the name of Jesus.
6. Every evil gathering against my destiny, be scattered, in the name of Jesus.
7. My destiny, you will not manage poverty, in the name of Jesus.
8. My destiny, you will not manage failure, in the name of Jesus.
9. I command my destiny to begin to change to the best now, in the name of Jesus.
10. My head will not carry evil load, in the name of Jesus.
11. Every enemy of progress in my life, fall down and die now, in the name

of Jesus.

12. I reject every evil manipulation against my destiny in every area of my life, in the name of Jesus.
13. I paralyse every activity of destiny killers in every area of my life, in the name of Jesus.
14. I smash every giant of 'almost there' to pieces, in Jesus' name.
15. I destroy every castle of backwardness, in the name of Jesus.
16. I receive the anointing to destroy every destiny killer, in the name of Jesus.
17. Let every satanic guard organised against my life be paralysed, in the name of Jesus.
18. I frustrate every evil network designed against my life, in the name of Jesus.
19. The enemies shall not understand the issues of my life, in the name of Jesus.
20. The enemies shall not understand the issues of my finances and blessings, in the name of Jesus.
21. Anything that has been done with the snail to slow down my life, be destroyed by the blood of Jesus, in the name of Jesus.
22. I reject every spirit of backwardness, in the name of Jesus.
23. I reject every caged life, in the name of Jesus.
24. I reject caged finances, in the name of Jesus.
25. I reject every caged health, in the name of Jesus.
26. I reject every caged marriage, in the name of Jesus.
27. I reject every spirit of stagnation, in the name of Jesus.
28. Every satanic chain on my legs, break now, in the name of Jesus.
29. Let every hole in my hand be blocked by the blood of Jesus, in the name of Jesus.
30. My life shall not be hung on the shelf, in the name of Jesus.

RULE NUMBER 69 - YOU MUST NOT SURRENDER NOR RETIRE

Joshua 14:10-14 says:

And now, behold, the LORD hath kept me alive, as he said, these forty and five years, even since the LORD spake this word unto Moses, while the children of Israel wandered in the wilderness: and now, lo, I am this day fourscore and five years old. As yet I am as strong this day as I was in the day that Moses sent me: as my strength was then, even so is my strength now, for war, both to go out, and to come in. Now therefore give me this mountain, whereof the LORD spake in that day; for thou heardest in that day how the Anakims were there, and that the cities were great and fenced: if so be the LORD will be with me, then I shall be able to drive them out, as the LORD said. And Joshua blessed him, and gave unto Caleb the son of Jephunneh Hebron for an inheritance. Hebron therefore became the inheritance of Caleb the son of Jephunneh the Kenezite unto this day, because that he wholly followed the LORD God of Israel.

Prayer Points

1. The enemy will not convert my destiny to rags, in Jesus' name.
2. Lord, lay Your hands of fire and change upon my destiny.
3. I reject and renounce destiny–demoting names and nullify their evil effects upon my destiny, in Jesus' name.
4. Any evil record against my destiny in the heavenlies as a result of destiny-demoting names, be wiped off by the blood of Jesus.
5. I refuse to operate below my divine destiny, in Jesus' name.
6. Every power contending with my divine destiny, scatter, in the name of Jesus.
7. Lord, change my destiny to the best that will dumbfound my enemies.
8. Satan, I resist and rebuke your efforts to change my destiny, in the name of Jesus.
9. Satan, I remove from you the right to rob me of my divine destiny, in the name of Jesus.

10. I command all powers of darkness assigned to my destiny to leave and never to return, in the name of Jesus.
11. The desire of my enemy against my destiny will not be granted in the heavenlies, in the name of Jesus.
12. The designs of my enemy against my destiny shall be destroyed, in the name of Jesus.
13. The deposits of my enemies in the heavenlies against my destiny shall be destroyed, in the name of Jesus.
14. The destiny of my enemy shall not be my lot, in Jesus' name.
15. Whether Satan likes it or not, I awake. to my destiny by fire, in the name of Jesus.
16. 0 Lord, give me new eyes to see into my destiny, in Jesus' name.
17. Conspiracy of darkness against my destiny, scatter by fire, in the name of Jesus.
18. The fire of the enemy against my destiny shall backfire, in Jesus' name.

RULE NUMBER 70 - CONNECT YOURSELF TO THE RESURRECTION POWER

Phil 3:10 says:

That I may know him, and the power of his resurrection, and the fellowship of his sufferings, being made conformable unto his death.

The Bible says, "That I may know him and the power of his resurrection." That power that raised Jesus from the dead is the resurrection power. Even if you are injured in the battle, connect yourself to His resurrection power and things will change.

Prayer Points

1. Every power of familiar spirit on my destiny, die, in Jesus' name.
2. Every power cursing my destiny, die, in the name of Jesus.
3. Every witchcraft incantation against my destiny, die, in Jesus' name.

4. Every wicked spirit assigned against my destiny, fail and fall by fire, in the name of Jesus.
5. Every serpent and scorpion working against my destiny, dry up and die, in the name of Jesus.
6. Every altar speaking against my divine destiny, be dismantled, in the name of Jesus.
7. Every attack against my destiny when I was a child, be destroyed, in the name of Jesus.
8. Every evil arrow fired against my destiny, fall down and die, in the name of Jesus.
9. Every satanic prayer against my destiny, be reversed, in Jesus' name
10. I withdraw satan's prayer against my destiny, in Jesus' name.
11. Let the vulture of judgment destroy the Pharaoh of my destiny, in the name of Jesus.
12. Let my destiny overshadow witchcraft envy, in Jesus' name.
13. Holy Ghost, let Your firing squad shot down every evil bird working against my destiny, in the name of Jesus.
14. Every satanic investment upon my destiny, scatter, in the name of Jesus.
15. My destiny, reject poverty, in the name of Jesus.
16. I forbid evil hands to perform their enterprise upon my destiny, in the name of Jesus.

TOTAL VICTORY

The rules of spiritual warfare in this life-changing book will transform your life as you use them after reading this book. Every effort made in the realm of warfare will surely yield great dividends. There is no doubt, that this is the moment of victory in your spiritual warfare. This is the season when you will practically experience the fulfilment of every prophesy in the area of spiritual warfare.

Roman 16:20 says:

And the God of peace shall bruise Satan under your feet shortly. The grace of our Lord Jesus Christ be with you. Amen.

Psalm 149:5-9 says:

Let the saints be joyful in glory: let them sing aloud upon their beds. Let the high praises of God be in their mouth, and a twoedged sword in their hand; To execute vengeance upon the heathen, and punishments upon the people; To bind their kings with chains, and their nobles with fetters of iron; To execute upon them the judgment written: this honour have all his saints. Praise ye the LORD.

Finally, to experience continued victory, you must use this book regularly.

Your victory shall remain unchallengeable.

Prayer Points

1. Let the spirit of prophesy and revelation fall upon the totally of my being, in the name of Jesus.
2. Holy Spirit, reveal deep and secret things to me about. . . , in the name of. Jesus.
3. I bind every demon that pollutes my spiritual vision and dreams, in the name of Jesus.
4. Let every dirt blocking my communication pipe with the living God be washed clean with the blood of Jesus, in Jesus' name.
5. I receive power to operate with sharp spiritual eyes that cannot be deceived, in the name of Jesus.
6. Let the glory and the power of the Almighty God, fall upon my life in a mighty way, in the name of Jesus.
7. I remove my name from the book of those who grope and stumble in darkness, in the name of Jesus.
8. Divine revelations, spiritual visions, dreams and information will not become scare commodities in my life, in the name of Jesus.
9. I drink to the full from the well of salvation and anointing, in the name of Jesus.
10. God, to whom no secret is hidden, make known unto me whether (mention the name of the thing) is Your choice for me, in the name of .Jesus.
11. Let every idol presence in my heart concerning this issue be melted away by the fire of the Holy Spirit, in the name of Jesus.
12. I refuse to fall under the manipulation of the spirit of confusion, in the name of Jesus.
13. I refuse to make foundational mistakes in my decision, in the name of Jesus.

14. Father Lord, guide arid direct me to know Your mind on this particular issue, in the name of Jesus.

15. I stand against all satanic attachments that may seek to confuse my decision, in the name of Jesus.

OTHER BOOKS BY DR. D. K. OLUKOYA

1. 20 Marching Orders To Fulfill Your Destiny
2. 30 Things The Anointing Can Do For You
3. A-Z of Complete Deliverance
4. Abraham's Children In Bondage
5. Be Prepared
6. Bewitchment must die
7. Biblical Principles of Dream Interpretation
8. Born Great, But Tied Down
9. Breaking Bad Habits
10. Breakthrough Prayers For Business Professionals
11. Brokenness
12. Bringing Down The Power of God
13. Can God?
14. Can God Trust You?
15. Command The Morning
16. Consecration Commitment & Loyalty
17. Contending For The Kingdom
18. Connecting to The God of Breakthroughs
19. Criminals In The House Of God
20. Dancers At The Gate of Death
21. Dealing With Hidden Curses
22. Dealing With Local Satanic Technology
23. Dealing With Satanic Exchange
24. Dealing With The Evil Powers Of Your Father's House
25. Dealing With Tropical Demons
26. Dealing With Unprofitable Roots
27. Dealing With Witchcraft Barbers
28. Deliverance By Fire
29. Deliverance From Spirit Husband And Spirit Wife

30. Deliverance From The Limiting Powers
31. Deliverance of The Brain
32. Deliverance Of The Conscience
33. Deliverance Of The Head
34. Deliverance: God's Medicine Bottle
35. Destiny Clinic
36. Destroying Satanic Masks
37. Disgracing Soul Hunters
38. Divine Military Training
39. Divine Yellow Card
40. Dominion Prosperity
41. Drawers Of Power From The Heavenlies
42. Evil Appetite
43. Evil Umbrella
44. Facing Both Ways
45. Failure In The School Of Prayer
46. Fire For Life's Journey
47. For We Wrestle ...
48. Freedom Indeed
49. Holiness Unto The Lord
50. Holy Cry
51. Holy Fever
52. Hour Of Decision
53. How To Obtain Personal Deliverance
54. How To Pray When Surrounded By The Enemies
55. Idols Of The Heart
56. Is This What They Died For?
57. Killing The Serpent of Frustration
58. Let God Answer By Fire
59. Lord, Behold Their Threatening

60. Limiting God
61. Madness Of The Heart
62. Making Your Way Through The Traffic Jam of Life
63. Meat For Champions
64. Medicine For Winners
65. My Burden For The Church
66. Open Heavens Through Holy Disturbance
67. Overpowering Witchcraft
68. Paralysing The Riders And The Horse
69. Personal Spiritual Check-Up
70. Possessing The Tongue of Fire
71. Power Against Coffin Spirits
72. Power Against Destiny Quenchers
73. Power Against Dream Criminals
74. Power Against Local Wickedness
75. Power Against Marine Spirits
76. Power Against Spiritual Terrorists
77. Power To Recover Your Lost Glory
78. Power Must Change Hands
79. Pray Your Way To Breakthroughs
80. Prayer Is The Battle
81. Prayer Rain
82. Prayer Strategies For Spinsters And Bachelors
83. Prayer To Kill Enchantment
84. Prayer To Make You Fulfill Your Divine Destiny
85. Prayer Warfare Against 70 Mad Spirits
86. Prayers For Open Heavens
87. Prayers To Destroy Diseases And Infirmities
88. Prayers To Move From Minimum To Maximum
89. Praying Against The Spirit Of The Valley

150. War At The Edge Of Breakthroughs
151. Wasting The Wasters
152. Wasted At The Market Square of Life
153. Wealth Must Change Hands
154. What You Must Know About The House Fellowship
155. When God Is Silent
156. When the Battle is from Home
157. When The Deliverer Need Deliverance
158. When Things Get Hard
159. When You Are Knocked Down
160. Where Is Your Faith
161. While Men Slept
162. Woman! Thou Art Loosed.
163. Your Battle And Your Strategy
164. Your Foundation And Destiny
165. Your Mouth And Your Deliverance

YORUBA PUBLICATIONS

1. ADURA AGBAYORI
2. ADURA TI NSI OKE NIDI
3. OJO ADURA

FRENCH PUBLICATIONS

1. PLUIE DE PRIERE
2. ESPIRIT DE VAGABONDAGE
3. EN FINIR AVEC LES FORCES MALEFIQUES DE LA MAISON DE TON PERE
4. QUE l'ENVOUTEMENT PERISSE
5. FRAPPEZ l'ADVERSAIRE ET IL FUIRA

6. COMMENT RECEVIOR LA DELIVRANCE DU MARI ET FEMME DE NUIT
7. CPMMENT SE DELIVRER SOI-MEME
8. POVOIR CONTRE LES TERRORITES SPIRITUEL
9. PRIERE DE PERCEES POUR LES HOMMES D'AFFAIRES
10. PRIER JUSQU'A REMPORTER LA VICTOIRE
11. PRIERES VIOLENTES POUR HUMILIER LES PROBLEMES OPINIATRES
12. PRIERE POUR DETRUIRE LES MALADIES ET INFIRMITES
13. LE COMBAT SPIRITUEL ET LE FOYER
14. BILAN SPIRITUEL PERSONNEL
15. VICTOIRES SUR LES REVES SATANIQUES
16. PRIERES DE COMAT CONTRE 70 ESPIRITS DECHANINES
17. LA DEVIATION SATANIQUE DE LA RACE NOIRE
18. TON COMBAT ET TA STRATEGIE
19. VOTRE FONDEMENT ET VOTRE DESTIN
20. REVOQUER LES DECRETS MALEFIQUES
21. CANTIQUE DES CONTIQUES
22. LE MAUVAIS CRI DES IDOLES
23. QUAND LES CHOSES DEVIENNENT DIFFICILES
24. LES STRATEGIES DE PRIERES POUR LES CELIBATAIRES
25. SE LIBERER DES ALLIANCES MALEFIQUES
26. DEMANTELER LA SORCELLERIE
27. LA DELIVERANCE: LE FLACON DE MEDICAMENT DIEU
28. LA DELIVERANCE DE LA TETE
29. COMMANDER LE MATIN
30. NE GRAND MAIS LIE
31. POUVOIR CONTRE LES DEMOND TROPICAUX
32. LE PROGRAMME DE TRANFERT DE RICHESSE
33. LES ETUDIANTS A l'ECOLE DE LA PEUR
34. L'ETOILE DANS VOTRE CIEL
35. LES SAISONS DE LA VIE

36. FEMME TU ES LIBEREE

ANNUAL 70 DAYS PRAYER AND FASTING PUBLICATIONS

1. Prayers That Bring Miracles
2. Let God Answer By Fire
3. Prayers To Mount With Wings As Eagles
4. Prayers That Bring Explosive Increase
5. Prayers For Open Heavens
6. Prayers To Make You Fulfil Your Divine Destiny
7. Prayers That Make God To Answer And Fight By Fire
8. Prayers That Bring Unchallengeable Victory And Breakthrough Rainfall Bombardments
9. Prayers That Bring Dominion Prosperity And Uncommon Success
10. Prayers That Bring Power And Overflowing Progress
11. Prayers That Bring Laughter And Enlargement Breakthroughs
12. Prayers That Bring Uncommon Favour And Breakthroughs
13. Prayers That Bring Unprecedented Greatness & Unmatchable Increase
14. Prayers That Bring Awesome Testimonies And Turn Around Breakthroughs

The Book

70 Rules of Spiritual Warfare is an indispensable manual. This book emits fire. It is a classic which everyone, involved in spiritual warfare will treasure in these end times. The exposition of these tested and proven rules is a product of thorough research by a spiritual warfare expert who has blazed the trail as a global phenomenon in the field of deliverance and spiritual warfare.

The rules will prove efficacious with application. The prayer points embedded in this compendium will produce fantastic results. It is handy, well articulated and prophetic. This is an invaluable companion for everyone whose passion is unchallengeable victory.

The Author

Dr. D. K. Olukoya is the General Overseer of the Mountain of Fire and Miracles Ministries and The Battle Cry Chrisitan Ministries.

The Mountain of Fire and Miracles Ministries' Headquarters is the largest single christian congregation in Africa with attendance of over 120,000 in single meetings.

MFM is a full gospel ministry devoted to the revival of Apostolic signs, Holy Ghost Fireworks, miracles and the unlimited demonstration of the power of God to deliver to the uttermost. Absolute holiness within and without as spiritual insecticide and pre-requisite for heaven is openly taught. MFM is a do-it-yourself Gospel Ministry, where your hands are trained to wage war and your fingers to do battle.

Dr. Olukoya holds a first class honours degree in Micro-biology from the University of Lagos and a PhD in Molecular Genetics from the University of Reading, United Kingdom. As a researcher, he has over seventy scientific publications to his credit.

Anointed by God, Dr. Olukoya is a prophet, evangelist, teacher and preacher of the Word. His life and that of his wife, Shade and their son, Elijah Toluwani are living proofs that all power belongs to God.

ISBN 978-978-8424-21-6

Made in the USA
Middletown, DE
05 February 2024

49088220R00089